Silver Burdett Ginn

Mathematics

Daily
Review

Practice

Problem Solving

Mixed Review

5

Silver Burdett Ginn
Parsippany, NJ

Atlanta, GA • Deerfield, IL • Irving, TX • Needham, MA • Upland, CA

Silver Burdett Ginn
A Division of Simon & Schuster
299 Jefferson Road, P.O. Box 480
Parsippany, NJ 07054-0480

1999 Printing

ISBN 0-382-37320-0

4 5 6 7 8 9-PO-00 99 98

Contents

EXPLORE: Understanding One Billion

1. There are one million sheets of paper in 2,000 reams. How many reams would be needed to have one billion sheets?

_____

Fill in the missing information in the table. Then answer the questions.

2. At about what age will a person have lived one million seconds?

_____

3. At about what age will a person have lived one billion seconds?

_____

Time	Number of Seconds
minute	60
hour	3,600
day	86,400
week	
30 days	

Problem Solving

4. Suppose there are 100 dog biscuits in one bag. How many bags would you need to have 1 billion dog biscuits?

_____

5. An airplane trip around the world is about 25,000 miles. How many trips would you have to make to earn one billion frequent-flyer miles?

_____

Review and Remember

Solve.

6. $48 \div 6 =$ ____   **7.** $8 \times 8 =$ ____   **8.** $63 \div 7 =$ ____   **9.** $42 + 18 =$ ____

10. $97 - 38 =$ _____   **11.** $9 \times 7 =$ _____   **12.** $181 + 17 =$ _____

13. $\begin{array}{r} 56 \\ +\ 44 \\ \hline \end{array}$ **14.** $\begin{array}{r} \$8.50 \\ -\ 2.50 \\ \hline \end{array}$ **15.** $\begin{array}{r} 397 \\ +\ 89 \\ \hline \end{array}$ **16.** $\begin{array}{r} 831 \\ -\ 200 \\ \hline \end{array}$

Name _____

Place Value to Billions

Write the value of the underlined digit.

1. 5,6<u>2</u>0   **2.** <u>6</u>08,423   **3.** <u>1</u>,432,556   **4.** 48,2<u>7</u>7

_____   _____   _____   _____

Write each in expanded form and short word form.

5. 11,435 _____

_____

Write in standard form.

6. 6000 + 400 + 20 + 8   **7.** 70,000 + 9,000 + 800

_____   _____

Problem Solving

8. What number am I? My millions digit is 4. My billions digit is two times my millions digit. My hundred thousands digit is two more than my millions digit and three more than my ones digit. My ten millions digit is one less than my ones digit. My other

digits are zero. Write my short word form. _____

_____

9. Write a number puzzle of your own. Exchange puzzles with a classmate.

_____

Review and Remember

Write a fact family for each set of numbers.

10. 6, 17, 23   **11.** 8, 9, 17   **12.** 6, 8, 14

_____   _____   _____

_____   _____   _____

_____   _____   _____

Comparing and Ordering Whole Numbers

Compare. Write >, <, or = .

1. 593 $\bigcirc$ 647

2. 6,606 $\bigcirc$ 6,666

3. 8,762 $\bigcirc$ 8,876

4. 364,523 $\bigcirc$ 364,523

5. 1,238,006,481 $\bigcirc$ 1,238,006,480

Order each set of numbers from least to greatest.

6. 138   152   125

7. 49,783   49,873   48,973

_____ , _____ , _____

_____ , _____ , _____

Order this set of numbers from greatest to least.

8. 1,483,625   1,488,625   1,483,725

_____ _____ _____

What comes next?

9. 3, 7, 11, _____ , _____ , 23

10. 1,538; _____ ; 1,536; 1,535

Problem Solving

11. Mr. Jones wants his basketball team to line up with the shortest player first and the tallest player last. In what order will they line up?

_____

_____

12. Estimate the difference in height between the tallest player and the shortest player on the team.

_____

Player	Height
Jose	5' 2"
Michael	6' 3"
Ian	5' 9"
Pedro	5' 9$\frac{1}{2}$"
Joseph	6'
Kenyon	5' 10"
Jason	5' 3"
Victor	5' 2$\frac{1}{2}$"

Review and Remember

Solve.

13. $17 - 8 =$ _____

14. $15 + 6 =$ _____

15. $8 \times 7 =$ _____

16. $13 \times 1 =$ _____

17. $64 \div 8 =$ _____

18. $5 \times 5 =$ _____

Rounding Whole Numbers

Round each number to the underlined place.

1. 6,2̲31

2. 44̲5

3. 47̲,498

4. 9̲8,014

_____ _____ _____ _____

Round each number to the nearest ten thousand.

5. 13,642

6. 48,289

7. 25,314

8. 991,289

_____ _____ _____ _____

Round each number to the nearest billion.

9. 2,004,837,621

10. 1,499,839,014

_____ _____

11. 999,300,489

12. 3,587,621,589

_____ _____

Problem Solving

Use the table to answer Problems 13–14.

13. About how much money would you need to buy a sofa, two chairs, three tables, and two lamps? Round to the

nearest hundred. _____

14. How much change would you expect to get from $200

if you purchased a table? _____

Woods Furniture	
Sofa	$899
Chair	$149
Table	$119
Lamp	$69

Review and Remember

Use mental math to solve.

15. $3.00 + $3.00 + $3.00 = _____

16. 15 ÷ 5 = _____

17. 16 − 9 = _____

18. $4.00 × 5 = _____

19. 7 × 7 = _____

20. 17 + 23 = _____

Problem Solving
Exact and Estimated Data

Read the paragraph and answer each question.

The sun is an average size star, and is about 1 million times larger than Earth. Earth is about 93,000,000 miles from the sun. It takes about 8 minutes for light from the sun to reach Earth. The next closest star to Earth is Alpha Centauri. It is over 4 light-years away from Earth.

1. Which phrase tells how large the sun is?

   a. about 1 million times larger than Earth

   b. over 4 light-years from Earth

   c. 93,000,000 miles to Earth

2. How long does it take light to reach Earth from the sun?

   a. 93,000,000 miles

   b. about 8 minutes

   c. over 4 years

3. How far is Alpha Centauri from Earth?

   a. less than 4 light-years

   b. more than 4 light-years

   c. exactly 4 light-years

4. Which of the numbers in the paragraph is an estimate?

_____

Review and Remember

Find the answer.

5. $19 + 21 =$ _____   **6.** $4 \times 6 =$ _____   **7.** $17 - 8 =$ _____   **8.** $20 \div 5 =$ _____

9. $56 \div 8 =$ _____   **10.** $9 \times 3 =$ _____   **11.** $53 + 47 =$ _____ **12.** $24 - 13 =$ _____

Understanding Decimal Place Value

What part is shaded?

1.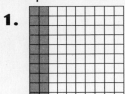

2.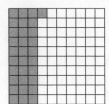

3.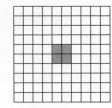

_____   _____   _____

Use grid paper to show:

4. 0.24   **5.** 2.4   **6.** 0.49   **7.** 0.01

8. the number of hundredths in one tenth

9. the number of tenths in thirty hundredths

Problem Solving

10. Is five tenths the same as fifty hundredths? Explain. _____

_____

_____

11. What decimal number is shown by these drawings? Explain your answer.

_____

_____

   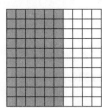

Review and Remember

Write the place value of each underlined digit.

12. 1<u>4</u>,816   **13.** 1,0<u>3</u>9   **14.** 4,5<u>0</u>9,861,234

_____   _____   _____

15. 86,45<u>3</u>   **16.** 4,<u>6</u>34   **17.** <u>6</u>,834,612

_____   _____   _____

Place Value to Thousandths

Write each decimal in standard form.

1. three thousandths

_____

2. five and five hundredths

_____

3. forty hundredths

_____

4. two hundred fifteen thousandths

_____

Write the word form for each decimal.

5. 0.9 _____

6. 102.08 _____

7. 0.300 _____

8. 2.020 _____

Write the value of each underlined digit.

9. 4.80<u>4</u> _____

10. 1<u>6</u>.015 _____

11. 0.<u>5</u>06 _____

12. 16.3<u>4</u>8 _____

Problem Solving

13. Study the decimal numbers shown in the table. If the pattern continues, what numbers would you expect to see next for Thursday and Friday?

_____

14. On what day of the week would you expect to reach a number greater than 2.00?

_____

Monday	1.78
Tuesday	1.81
Wednesday	1.84
Thursday	
Friday	

Review and Remember

Compare. Write $>$, $<$, or $=$.

15. $7 + 7 + 7$ ◯ 3×7

16. 2×3 ◯ $2 + 3$

17. 4×3 ◯ 3×4

18. 7×8 ◯ 7×9

19. 2×2 ◯ $2 + 2$

20. 10×8 ◯ 10×7

Use with Grade 5, text pages 20-21. **7**

Comparing and Ordering Decimals

Compare. Write >, <, or =.

1. 3.42 $\bigcirc$ 3.85   **2.** 2.4 $\bigcirc$ 2.004   **3.** 4.3 $\bigcirc$ 4.30

4. 0.08 $\bigcirc$ 0.80   **5.** 68.4 $\bigcirc$ 68.04   **6.** 7.01 $\bigcirc$ 7.010

Order from least to greatest.

7. 0.45, 0.54, 0.46   **8.** 1.003, 0.04, 1.04

_____, _____, _____   _____, _____, _____

9. 3.89, 3.98, 3.891   **10.** 1.01, 1.11, 1.001, 1.10

_____, _____, _____   _____, _____, _____, _____

Problem Solving

Use the chart to answer Problems 11–12.

11. Name the month when the temperature in New York is closest to the temperature in Miami.

_____

12. For the average temperatures shown for Miami, order the months from warmest to coolest.

_____

Average Temperature		
	Miami	New York
January	67.1°F	31.8°F
April	75.3°F	51.9°F
July	82.5°F	76.4°F
October	77.9°F	57.5°F

Review and Remember

Write the place value of each underlined digit.

13. 14.5̲67 _____   **14.** 24̲5.508 _____

15. 23̲.406 _____   **16.** 283.48̲9 _____

Round off to the place value underlined.

17. 1̲6,532 _____   **18.** 1̲.33 _____

19. 10̲,003 _____   **20.** 453,6̲29,941 _____

Problem Solving
Draw a Diagram

Use the diagram at the right to answer Problems 1–2.

1. Mr. Coleman is building a brick patio. He completes the first 6 feet of the patio in the morning. How many more feet does he have to build? _____

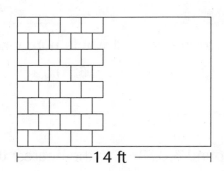

—— 14 ft ——

2. If Mr. Coleman wants to double the width of his patio, how wide will the new patio be?

_____

Draw diagrams to answer Problems 3–5.

3. A tour bus travels 2 blocks due north, 3 blocks due east, 4 blocks due south, 9 blocks due west, and 2 blocks due north. Where is the bus in relation to its starting point?

_____

4. Jason got on the elevator at ground level. The elevator went up 15 floors, down 3 floors, up 5 floors, down 10 floors, and down 2 more floors. What floor is Jason on?

_____

5. Justin is making a track for his model train. He has three pieces of track laid end to end. One piece is 2 times the length of the shortest piece. The longest piece is 4 times the length of the shortest piece. If the shortest piece is 10 inches long, how long is the track? _____

Review and Remember

Find the answer.

6. $1.89 + $0.59

_____

7. $5.98 − $1.35

_____

8. $6.00 − $2.50

_____

9. $5.00 × 3

_____

10. $25.05 + $3.15 + $4.05

_____

11. $20.00 ÷ 5

_____

Rounding Decimals

Round each number to the underlined place.

1. 2.3̲8   **2.** 0.003̲4   **3.** 0.8̲84   **4.** 1.99̲5

_____   _____   _____   _____

Round to the nearest whole number.

5. 4.73   **6.** 0.59   **7.** 19.6   **8.** 13.09

_____   _____   _____   _____

9. Round 5.07345 to the nearest thousandth. _____

10. Round 458.243 to the nearest tenth. _____

11. Round 3.776 to the nearest hundredth. _____

Problem Solving

Use the table to answer Problems 12–13.

12. About how much money is needed to buy a loaf of bread, a gallon of milk, 2 pounds of ground beef, and one gallon of ice cream?

_____

13. If you bought a dozen apples, how much change would you expect to receive from a five-dollar bill?

_____

Jillian's Market	
bread	$1.09 per loaf
milk	$1.49 per gal
ground beef	$1.99 per lb
ice cream	$2.09 per half gal
apples	3 for $0.49

Review and Remember

Compare. Write $>$, $<$, or $=$.

14. 6.08 $\bigcirc$ 6.008   **15.** 156 $\bigcirc$ 15.6   **16.** 3.40 $\bigcirc$ 3.4

17. 10.01 $\bigcirc$ 100.1   **18.** 46.3 $\bigcirc$ 46.30   **19.** 4.025 $\bigcirc$ 4.052

20. 0.07 $\bigcirc$ 0.007   **21.** 510.0 $\bigcirc$ 510.01   **22.** 88.08 $\bigcirc$ 88.080

Problem Solving

Using Tables and Graphs

Use the "Star Colors and Temperatures" table and graph to answer Problems 1–3.

Star Colors and Temperatures	
Color	Temperature
red	A
C	6,000°C
white	7,000°C
blue	B

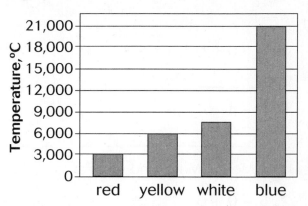

1. Provide the missing information for A, B, and C. _____

2. How many times hotter is a blue star than a red star? _____

3. The sun is a yellow star. About what temperature is the sun? _____

Use the graph to answer Problems 4–5.

Length of Playing Areas

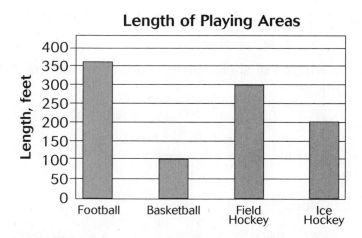

4. Which sport is played on the longest area? _____

5. How much longer is an ice hockey rink than a basketball court? _____

Review and Remember

Compare. Use >, <, or =.

6. 1,246 ◯ 1,426   **7.** 348 ◯ 338   **8.** 13 – 6 ◯ 14 – 5   **9.** 4 ◯ 4.00

Working With Addition Properties

Find each *n*. Name the property used.

1. (5 + 3) + 2 = 5 + (3 + *n*)

_____

2. 14 + *n* = 14

_____

3. 6 + 0 + *n* = 6 + 2 + 0

_____

4. *n* + (5 + 7) = (6 + 5) + 7

_____

5. 9 + 4 = *n* + 9

_____

6. *n* + 0 = 81

_____

Using Mental Math, find each sum.

7. 5 + 0 + 6 = _____

8. 14 + 6 + 20 = _____

9. 12 + 9 + 8 = _____

Problem Solving

10. Alyssa collects seashells during the summer.
In June, she collected 25 shells.
In July, she collected 89 shells.
In August, she collected 75 shells. How many shells did Alyssa collect in all?

_____

11. If Alyssa collects the same amount of shells each summer, about how many shells will she collect in three summers?

_____

Review and Remember

Round to the underlined place value.

12. <u>1</u>89

_____

13. 4,8<u>6</u>0

_____

14. 690,<u>3</u>45

_____

15. 9,8<u>9</u>5

_____

16. <u>3</u>5

_____

17. 487,<u>6</u>34,218

_____

18. 13.<u>4</u>86

_____

19. 1.04<u>5</u>3

_____

20. 245.8<u>9</u>13

_____

Mental Math: Using Compatible Numbers and Compensation

Use Mental Math. Find each sum or difference.

1. 13 + 7 + 19 = _____   **2.** 42 − 17 = _____   **3.** 52 + 17 + 10 = _____

4. 43 −23 = _____   **5.** 50 + 25 + 50 = _____   **6.** 64 − 59 = ___

7. 111 + 100 + 19 = _____   **8.** 32 + 19 + 68 = _____

9. 1 + 26 + 4 + 19 = _____   **10.** 97 − 58 = _____

Problem Solving

11. Use compensation to subtract 184 and 69. Explain how you got your answer.

_____

12. The Junior League football team scored points in all four quarters of their game. Use compatible numbers and compensation to find their final score. Explain how you got your answer.

_____

_____

First	Second	Third	Fourth	Final Score
17	27	3	28	

Review and Remember

Solve.

13. 99 + 99 = _____   **14.** 1.7 − 0.8 = _____   **15.** 7 × 7 = _____

16. 45 ÷ 9 = _____   **17.** 492 − 163 = _____   **18.** 214 + 87.6 = _____

19. 8 × 0 = _____   **20.** 112 + 79 = _____   **21.** 72 ÷ 8 = _____

Relating Addition and Subtraction

Find each input or output.

Rule: Add 31	
Input	**Output**
1. 29	
2.	62
3. 159	

Rule: Subtract 25	
Input	**Output**
4.	75
5. 25	
6.	130

Find the rule for each input/output table.

7.

Rule: _____	
Input	**Output**
6	6
113	113
159	159

8.

Rule: _____	
Input	**Output**
30	45
45	60
60	75

Problem Solving

Suppose juice drinks from a vending machine cost 65 cents. Design an input/output table that helps you find out how much change you would receive from each combination of money.

9. three quarters _____

10. two quarters, and two dimes _____

11. two quarters, one dime, and one nickel _____

Rule: _____	
Input	**Output**
9.	
10.	
11.	

Review and Remember

Round each number to the hundreds place.

12. 149   **13.** 2,859   **14.** 456,345   **15.** 249

_____   _____   _____   _____

Round each number to the tens place.

16. 45.865   **17.** 6,834   **18.** 25.19   **19.** 74,582

_____   _____   _____   _____

Problem Solving

Is an Estimate Enough?

Answer each question. Give a reason for your choice.

Michael and Brian are meeting at the library. Michael is riding his bicycle.
He rides at about 2 miles per 10 minutes. Brian is walking. He walks at
about 4 miles per hour.

1. What do you need to know to find exactly out how long it will take
Michael to reach the library?

    a. An estimate of the distance to the library
and the exact bicycle speed

    b. An exact distance to the library and an
estimated bicycle speed

    c. An exact distance to the library and an
exact bicycle speed

2. Which expression shows Michael's estimated speed in miles per hour?

    a. 2 mi per 10 min ÷ 60 min

    b. (60 min ÷ 10 min) × 2

    c. (2 mi × 60 min) ÷ 10

3. What best describes how to find how long it will take Michael
to reach the library?

    a. distance ÷ 12 mph

    b. distance + 1 mile per 5 min

    c. distance × 4 mph

Review and Remember

Round each number to the underlined place.

4. 6,5<u>3</u>8   **5.** 1,34<u>8</u>,006   **6.** 486,<u>1</u>92   **7.** 32,9<u>9</u>5

_____   _____   _____   _____

8. <u>1</u>,234   **9.** <u>4</u>,652   **10.** 367,4<u>3</u>8   **11.** <u>2</u>8,436

_____   _____   _____   _____

Using Rounding to Estimate

Estimate by rounding to the greatest place.

1. 866
$+ 659$ _____

2. 856
231
415
$+ 12$ _____

3. 6,487
$- 2,983$ _____

Use estimation and compare. Write $>$, $<$, or $=$.

4. $55 + 45 \bigcirc 35 + 65$

5. $55 - 12 \bigcirc 55 + 12$

6. $26 + 12 \bigcirc 24 + 18$

7. $27 + 113 \bigcirc 67 + 33$

8. $89 - 12 \bigcirc 55 + 111$

9. $133 - 122 \bigcirc 133 + 17$

Problem Solving

Solve. Use estimation.

10. Meghan's allowance is $2.50 per week. About how long will it take for her to save $20.00?

_____

11. Meghan wants to buy her sister a birthday present. She has $20.00 to spend. She plans to buy a CD for $14.99 and a ticket to the movies for $5.99. Does she have enough money? Explain your answer.

_____

Review and Remember

Find each n.

12. $16 + n = 3 + 16$

$n =$ _____

13. $(4 + 5) + 6 = n + (5 + 6)$

$n =$ _____

14. $n + 0 = 16$

$n =$ _____

Use compatible numbers to find each sum.

15. 14
16
$+ 13$

16. 15
8
22
$+ 15$

17. 11
189
121
$+ 89$

18. 26
13
4
$+ 87$

Using Front-End Estimation

Estimate each sum or difference using front-end estimation.
Then adjust to find a closer estimate.

1. 569 + 388 = _____

2. 58 + 34 + 18 = _____

3. 583 − 324 = _____

4. 625 − 489 = _____

5. 1.89 + 2.34 = _____

6. 23.09 + 45.62 = _____

7. 2.35 − 1.89 = _____

8. 24.53 − 11.09 = _____

9. 635 − 486 = _____

10. 400 − 159 = _____

11. 189 + 208 + 111 = _____

12. 456 + 382 + 401 = _____

Problem Solving

Use the table for Problems 13–14. Use front-end estimation.
Then adjust to find a closer estimate.

13. The chart shows the population of six of
the largest cities in the United States. About
how large is the total population of these cities?

_____

14. About how many more people live in
New York than in San Diego?

_____

Population of U.S. Cities	
New York	7,322,564
Los Angeles	3,485,398
Chicago	2,783,726
Houston	1,630,553
Philadelphia	1,585,577
San Diego	1,110,549

Review and Remember

Find each n.

15. $n + 20 = 100$

$n =$ _____

16. $33 + n + 40 = 100$

$n =$ _____

17. $45 − n = 25$

$n =$ _____

18. $3 \times n = 12$

$n =$ _____

19. $70 + 80 + n = 200$

$n =$ _____

20. $217 + 43 = n$

$n =$ _____

Problem Solving

Write an Equation

Write an equation for each problem and solve.

1. Jose is saving to buy a pair of in-line skates. He has saved $70.00. The skates cost $150.00. How much more does Joshua need to save?

_____

2. It takes Michelle 23 minutes to skate to Molly's house. If she plans to arrive at Molly's by 3:30 P.M., what time should Michelle leave her house?

_____

3. Joshua and his friends are raising money to help build a skateboard park. Joshua has raised $150.00, Felix has raised $130.00, Eric $75.00, and Kurt $200.00. How much money have they raised all together?

_____

4. It takes Tom twice as long to clean his room as it takes his sister to clean her room. If his sister takes 25 minutes to clean her room, how long does Tom take to clean his room?

_____

Review and Remember

Solve.

5. $6 \times 7 =$ _____

6. $3 \times 4 =$ _____

7. $7 \times 7 =$ _____

8. $5 \times 9 =$ _____

9. $15 \div 3 =$ _____

10. $24 \div 6 =$ _____

11. $24 \div 3 =$ _____

12. $18 \div 2 =$ _____

13. $128 + 128 =$ _____

14. $43 + 184 =$ _____

15. $77 - 48 =$ _____

16. $894 - 685 =$ _____

Adding and Subtracting Greater Whole Numbers

Add or subtract. Check your answer. Estimate by rounding to the greatest place.

1. 8,845
   + 2,689

2.   683
   + 25

3.   6, 152
   −   48

4. 26,835
  − 12,852

5.   8,945
  + 6,589

Find the missing digits.

6.   2☐3
   6 2☐
 +☐4 3
 ☐,0 5 2

7. 5 4☐
 − 1☐9
 ☐1 5

8. 5,☐2 8
 2, 3 9☐
 + 6, 2☐1
 1☐,1 1 1

9. 6,☐4 2
 − 1, 0 8☐
 ☐,9 6 1

10. ☐,4 3 2
 + 5, 0 8☐
 10, 5☐5

Problem Solving

Use the table for Problems 11–12.

11. Juan found the total depth of the Great Lakes to be 27,000 feet. Is his total reasonable? Explain.

_____

_____

Depth of Great Lakes (Feet)	
Huron	750
Ontario	802
Michigan	923
Erie	210
Superior	1,333

12. What is the total depth of the Great Lakes? _____

Review and Remember

Write the word name for each number.

13. 16,000,000

14. 1,001,001,001

15. 1.06

16. 10.013

17. 200,200

18. 45.40

Name _____

Explore: Adding and Subtracting Decimals

Use grid paper to find each sum.

1. 1.3 + 2.4 = ———   **2.** 3.67 + 1.4 = ———   **3.** 1.48 + 2.97 = ———

Use grid paper to find each difference.

4. 3.24 − 1.11 = ———   **5.** 5.23 − 1.75 = ———   **6.** 5 − 2.3 = ———

7. Write the correct addition sentence for this set of shaded grids. Then solve.

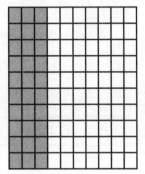 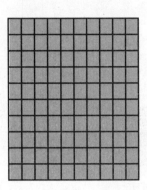 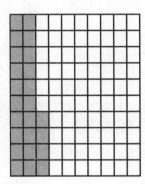

_____

Problem Solving

8. Sally has $6.53 in coins in her piggy bank. She has 17 quarters, 12 dimes, and 9 nickels. How many pennies are in her bank? Use grid paper to check your answer.

_____

9. Write an addition sentence and a subtraction sentence for Problem 8.

_____

_____

Review and Remember

Use compatible numbers and compensations for each sum or difference.

10. 117 + 30 + 23 = ———   **11.** 41 − 27 = ———

12. 83 + 5 + 25 + 117 = ———   **13.** 232 − 127 = ———

Adding Decimals

Estimate for reasonableness. Then find each sum.

1. 2.34
       + 5.45 ____

2. 4.389
       + 2.480 ____

3. 2.900
       + 31.2 ____

4. 36.45
       + 44.00 ____

5. 5.8 + 0.37 = _____

6. 8.347 + 2.33 = _____

7. 203.5 + 24.34 = _____

8. 4.79 + 8 = _____

Problem Solving

9. The school is buying equipment for a media center. They plan to purchase a large-screen television for $1,099.99, a CD player for $199.99, and a VCR for $239. How much do they plan to spend?

_____

10. How much greater is the price of the VCR than the price of the CD player?

_____

11. How much would it cost the school to purchase two additional CD players?

_____

Review and Remember

Round off to the place value underlined.

12. $14.95

_____

13. $8.05

_____

14. $145.69

_____

15. $1,999.99

_____

16. $435.56

_____

17. $289.55

_____

18. $149.00

_____

19. $149.00

_____

20. $2,089

_____

Name _____

Subtracting Decimals

Subtract.

1. 12.67
  − 1.25

2. 39.06
  − 9.95

3. 70.39
  − 25.46

4. $40.50
  − 6.17

5. $5.00 − $1.65 = _____

6. 7.8 − 4.3 = _____

7. 10 − 1.35 = _____

8. 1.9 − 0.0899 = _____

9. 24.083 − 1.39 = _____

10. 4.05 − 2.967 = _____

Problem Solving

The student council recently sponsored a dance. They spent $200.00 for a disc jockey and $145.69 for decorations and refreshments. They collected $800.00 from ticket sales.

11. What were their total expenses? _____

_____

12. How much profit did they make from the dance? _____

_____

Review and Remember

Find *n*.

13. 16 ÷ 4 = n

n = ____

14. 3 × n = 21

n = ____

15. 9 + n = 15

n = ____

16. n × 1 = 6

n = ____

17. 6 × n = 0

n = ____

18. n − 14 = 32

n = ____

19. n × n = 25

n = ____

20. 17 + n + 20 = 50

n = ____

21. 27 ÷ n = 3

n = ____

Adding and Subtracting Decimals

Find the exact sum or difference.

1. 2.36 + 3.78 + 2.67 = _____   **2.** 2.4 + 0.52 + 8 = _____

3. 6.83 − 2.9 = _____   **4.** 0.5 − 0.006 = _____

5. 5.36 − 0.289 = _____   **6.** 6 + 4.3 + 0.05 = _____

7. 6.23 − 4.9 = _____   **8.** 9 − 1.009 = _____

9. 6 − 4.58 = _____   **10.** 4.3 + 0.5 = _____

Problem Solving

Use the table for Problems 11–12.

11. What was the total amount of money spent by the cafeteria? Is your answer reasonable? Explain.

_____

_____

12. How much more did the cafeteria spend on meats and vegetables than it did on fruits and desserts?

_____

School Cafeteria Expenses	
meats	$568.15
vegetables	$235.89
fruits	$189.26
desserts	$179.35
breads	$165.85
milks	$158.39
other	$63.50

Review and Remember

Round each number to the highest place value. Then estimate the sum or difference.

13. 453
  − 148 _____

14. 3,892
  − 202 _____

15. 236
  459
  + 598 _____

16. 57
  2,708
  441
  + 259 _____

17. 6,583
  − 67 _____

18. 253
  + 899 _____

19. 403
  + 247 _____

20. 487
  − 385 _____

Choosing a Computation Method

Choose a method. Use Mental Math, paper and pencil, or a calculator to find each sum or difference. Tell which methods you used.

1. 56 + 44 = _____

2. 8.25 + 3.89 = _____

3.   1,382,465
     − 289,698

4. 5.63 − 2.81 = _____

5. $100 − $25 = _____

6.   548,631
     + 200,102

7. $189.99 + $67.49 + $3.45 = _____

8. 4,358 + 2,498 + 23,698 = _____

Problem Solving

Use the table for Problems 9–10. Explain the method you chose to answer each question.

9. Mr. Ramon wants to buy a new four-wheel drive truck. He has saved $8,000. How much more money will he need to buy the truck at the sticker price?

_____

10. Mr. Ramon will ask the dealer to include a luggage rack and a CD player. How much will these extras add to the price of the truck?

_____

The Truck Center	
New four-wheel drives $24,000.00	
Extra Options	**Cost**
Air Conditioning	$839.99
CD Player	$439.99
Luggage Rack	$279.99

Review and Remember

Find each n. Name the property used.

11. 6 − n = 6

12. 3.68 + 2.4 = n + 3.68

_____

_____

13. 863 − 0 = n

14. (258 + 345) + n = 258 + (345 + 9)

_____

_____

15. 4 + (1.8 + 0) = 4 + (n + 1.8)

16. 2,383 + (483 + n) = (2,383 + 483) + 17

_____

_____

Problem Solving
Using a Pictograph

Use the pictograph at the right to answer Problems 1–6.

1. How many T-shirts were sold each day?

_____

_____

2. Which day was the best day for sales?

_____

3. How many T-shirts were sold during the whole week?

_____

4. How many more T-shirts were sold on Saturday than on Wednesday?

_____

5. If T-shirts sold for $8.00 each, was there more than $2,500.00 in total sales? Explain.

_____

6. Use the pictograph on T-shirts to write your own word problem.

_____

Tower Hill T-Shirt Sales

Monday	👕
Tuesday	👕👕
Wednesday	👕👕
Thursday	👕👕
Friday	👕👕👕
Saturday	👕👕👕👕👕
Sunday	👕👕👕👕

👕 = 20 T-shirts

Review and Remember

Write the value of the underlined digit in short word form.

7. 6,4<u>2</u>8

8. 1,01<u>3</u>,482

9. <u>2</u>,468,932

10. <u>4</u>5,628

_____   _____   _____   _____

_____   _____   _____   _____

11. 2,<u>8</u>34,289

12. 4,<u>6</u>23

13. 1,09<u>3</u>

14. <u>1</u>2,633,425

_____   _____   _____   _____

EXPLORE: Collecting Data

Use the line plot and the frequency table for Problems 1–4.

1. How many people were surveyed?

_____

2. What kind of information is found in the line plot?

_____

3. What kind of information is found in the frequency table?

_____

4. Write an example of the type of question that a researcher may have asked students in this survey.

_____

5. Which do you find easier to read, a line plot or a frequency table? Explain your answer.

_____

Cafeteria Foods

```
                X
                X
        X       X
        X       X       X
        X       X       X
        X       X       X
        X       X       X
        X       X       X
        X       X       X
        X       X       X
      Tacos   Pizza   Burger
```

Cafeteria Foods	
Response	**Number**
Tacos	8
Pizza	10
Burgers	7

Problem Solving

6. Take a survey of thirty people. Ask them what month they were born in. Organize your data in a line plot and a frequency table. Then write a short paragraph that describes your data.

_____

7. Explain how a line plot and a frequency table help you analyze the data you collected in your survey.

_____

Review and Remember

Find each answer. Use Mental Math, pencil and paper, or a calculator.

8. $7 \times 7 =$ _____ **9.** $151 + 49 + 89 =$ _____ **10.** $\$9 + \$2.58 =$ _____

Double Bar Graphs

Use the data in the table at the right to make a double bar graph.

1. What is the title of your graph?

_____

2. What labels did you use for your axes?

_____

_____

3. What intervals did you use for the boxes of cookies?

_____

Use your graph to answer Problem 4.

4. Which girl sold the most cookies? How do you know? _____

_____

Boxes of Cookies Sold		
	Amy	Tiffany
Sunday	50	75
Monday	25	30
Tuesday	15	20
Wednesday	30	15
Thursday	30	30
Friday	70	50
Saturday	45	100

Problem Solving

Use the data in the bar graph at the right to answer Problems 5–7.

5. Estimate the number of minutes Jake worked out.

_____

6. Estimate the number of minutes Adam worked out.

_____

7. What comparison can you make about the amount of workout time for Adam and Jake each week?

_____

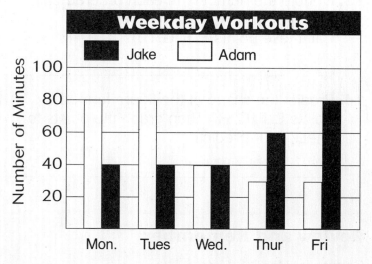

Review and Remember

Find the answer.

8. 23 × 3 = _____

9. 50 × 2 = _____

10. 10 × 10 = _____

11. 100 ÷ 2 = _____

12. 24 ÷ 3 = _____

13. 54 ÷ 6 = _____

Coordinate Graphing

Use the map on page 92 in your textbook.
Write the name of the state located by each ordered pair.

1. (1, 5)   **2.** (5, 5)   **3.** (9, 4)   **4.** (10, 6)   **5.** (4, 4)

_____   _____   _____   _____   _____

Write the ordered pair that locates each state.

6. Illinois   **7.** New Mexico   **8.** Pennsylvania   **9.** South Carolina   **10.** Utah

_____   _____   _____   _____   _____

Problem Solving

11. Use the grid at the right to graph these ordered pairs.

A (1, 2)   B (1, 3)   C (4, 3)   D (4, 2)

12. Draw a figure by connecting the four points.

What shape is formed? _____

13. Double the numbers in each ordered pair and write a new set of ordered pairs. Call these points E, F, G, H.

_____

14. Predict the shape of the figure formed by points E, F, G, H. Then graph the points to check your prediction.

_____

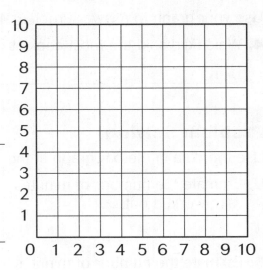

Review and Remember

Compare. Use >, <, or =.

15. 120 ◯ 120.1   **16.** 3.4 ◯ 3.400

17. 1908 ◯ 1898   **18.** 468.24 ◯ 14,680

19. 10.8 ◯ 10.08   **20.** 23 + 17 ◯ 40 − 10

Problem Solving

Understanding Line Graphs

Use the line graph below to answer Problems 1–5.

1. Which point shows the greatest number of games sold?

    a. A   **b.** F   **c.** L

2. At what point did sales first begin to increase?

    a. F   **b.** H   **c.** I

3. Which statement best describes what happened between points B and C?

    a. No games were sold.

    b. The number of games sold stayed the same.

    c. The number of games sold decreased.

Computer Game Sales

4. Which statement best describes the graph?

    a. Sales were poorest in August.

    b. No one buys computer games in May.

    c. More computer games were bought in the second half of the year.

5. What statement could you make about the sales in June? Explain.

_____

Review and Remember

Round each to the nearest tenth.

6. 2.38   **7.** 2.24   **8.** 36.093   **9.** 0.56

_____   _____   _____   _____

10. 16.054   **11.** 0.156   **12.** 9.998   **13.** 4.958

_____   _____   _____   _____

Reading Line Graphs

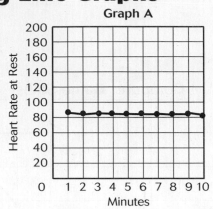

Graph A

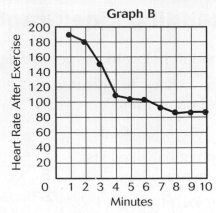

Graph B

Use Graph A and Graph B to answer these questions.

1. How much time is represented by each of these graphs?

_____

2. According to Graph A, what is this person's normal heart rate when at rest?

_____

3. Why do you think the line in Graph A is horizontal?

_____

4. How long does it take this person's heart rate to return to normal after exercise?

_____

5. Estimate the difference between the two heart rates at the one minute mark in each graph.

_____

Problem Solving

6. Why do you think retail business people would use line graphs to represent their sales

results over time? Explain. _____

7. On another sheet of paper draw an imaginary line graph that would show a very successful year in retail sales.

Review and Remember

Estimate. Then find the exact sum or difference.

8. 98.6 + 34.9 ____	**9.** 587.4 − 435.78 ____	**10.** 1508 − 1459 ____	**11.** 28.9 + 35.4 ____

EXPLORE: Making Line Graphs

Work with a partner and record each other's data.

1. Check your heart rate and have your partner fill in the top table at the right.

Heart Rate at Rest										
Rate										
Min	1	2	3	4	5	6	7	8	9	10

2. Do 5–10 minutes of light exercise. Then repeat Problem 1 for the bottom table.

3. Graph the data from each table on a line graph. Title each graph, label the axes, and set a scale of intervals.

Heart Rate After Exercise										
Rate										
Min	1	2	3	4	5	6	7	8	9	10

4. How are the two graphs the same? _____

5. How are the two graphs different? _____

Problem Solving

6. Use the data in the table at the right to draw a line graph.

7. What scale of intervals did you use for the temperature scale? Why?

_____

8. What is the difference between the lowest and the highest

average monthly temperatures? _____

9. What conclusion could you make about these average monthly temperatures?

_____

Month	Temp °F
J	22
F	28
M	31
A	39
M	46
J	53
J	56
A	55
S	49
O	42
N	43
D	27

Review and Remember

Use the grid at the right to write the ordered pair for each point.

10. J _____
11. G _____
12. E _____

13. B _____
14. H _____
15. C _____

16. A _____
17. I _____
18. F _____

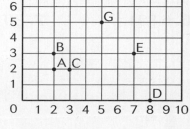

Problem Solving
Make a Graph

Use the data below for Problems 1–3.

Average Monthly Rainfall in Florida

Month	Jan.	Feb.	Mar.	April	May	June	July	Aug.	Sept.	Oct.	Nov.	Dec.
Inches	2.2	3.0	3.5	1.8	3.4	5.3	7.4	7.6	6.2	2.3	1.9	2.1

1. Make an appropriate graph to represent the average monthly rainfall in Florida.

2. According to your graph, which month has the lowest average rainfall?

_____

3. Between what months is the greatest decrease in average rainfall reported?

_____

Use the data to the right for Problems 4–5.

4. Make an appropriate graph to represent the data.

5. Which subject was the favorite of both groups?

_____

Favorite Subjects		
	Grade 5	**Grade 8**
English	19	39
Math	39	45
Science	45	36
Social Studies	45	30
Computers	52	50

Review and Remember

Write the value of the underlined digit in short word form.

6. 6.$\underline{8}$91 **7.** $\underline{3}$0.46 **8.** 25.18$\underline{2}$ **9.** 6.0$\underline{8}$3

_____ _____ _____ _____

Name _____

Graphs That Look Different

Use the graphs at the right for Problems 1–8.

1. What is the first thing you notice about the two graphs?

_____

_____

2. What are the intervals on each graph?

_____

3. About how much difference is there between the high and low test grade on each graph? _____

4. Which graph best shows that the test results were similar? Why?

_____

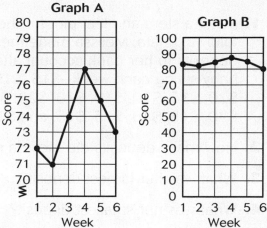

Graph A

Graph B

Problem Solving

5. What does this graph show about the test results for

this class? _____

6. How many students took the test? _____

7. How many students got below 70%? _____

8. How could you change the graph to make the test results

look more similar for all students? _____

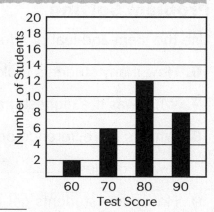

Review and Remember

Find each n.

9. $9 \times 9 = n$

$n =$ ___

10. $n \times n = 16$

$n =$ ___

11. $n \times n = 4$

$n =$ ___

12. $8 \times 7 = n$

$n =$ ___

13. $n \times n = 100$

$n =$ ___

14. $63 \div 7 = n$

$n =$ ___

Stem-and-Leaf Plots

Stem	Leaves

1. Make a stem-and-leaf plot for the
following data. Melissa made these
deposits to her bank account after
baby-sitting each week—$15, $19,
$20, $15, $10, $30, $18, $22, $23,
$20, $15, $18, $15, $15, and $15.

2. How many deposits did Melissa make? _____

3. What was her largest deposit? _____

4. What was her smallest deposit? _____

5. About how much money does she normally make each week? Explain.

_____

_____

Problem Solving

Use the stem-and-leaf plot for quiz grades to answer Problems 6–10.

6. How many students took the quiz? _____

7. What was the highest grade? _____

8. What is the difference between the highest and

lowest grades? _____

9. How many students got a grade of 75? _____

10. How many students got a grade higher than 75? _____

Stem	Leaves
6	2 3
7	3 5 5 5
8	2 5
9	0 5

Review and Remember

Find n.

11. $63 - 13 = n$

$n =$ ____

12. $24 \times 2 = n$

$n =$ ____

13. $658 + 42 = n$

$n =$ ____

14. $n \div 2 = 25$

$n =$ ____

15. $8 \times n = 0$

$n =$ ____

16. $1,435 \times n = 1,435$

$n =$ ____

Range, Mode, and Median

Find the range, median, and mode for each set of data.

1. 5, 1, 22, 18, 7, 7, 24

_____

2. 6, 15, 15, 16, 8

_____

3. $100, $20, $108, $701,
$108, $101, $40

_____

4. 26.7, 36.1, 29.3, 34.1,
37.4, 33.6, 36.1

_____

5. 71, 73, 74, 76, 78, 78, 79

_____

6. 55, 3, 2, 50, 2

_____

Use the table at the right to answer Problems 7–9.

7. Find the range, median, and mode of these
bowling scores. _____

8. What would the range be if the score of the
fourth string was changed to 197? _____

9. What would the mode be if the score of the
third string was changed to 147? _____

Bowling Scores	
String	Score
1	149
2	183
3	149
4	193
5	147

Problem Solving

Use the line graph at the right to answer these
problems.

10. How would you describe the team's bowling
average over time? _____

_____

11. Should a different interval have been used for
this graph? If so, what interval? _____

_____

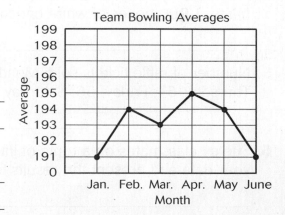

Review and Remember

Compare. Use >, <, or =.

12. 6 × 3 ◯ 6 × 4   **13.** 6 ÷ 2 ◯ 6 × 2   **14.** 144 + 6 ◯ 5 + 145

Problem Solving
Ways to Represent Data

Choose a way to organize and display the data in Problems 1–6.
Explain your choice.

1. Class scores on Chapter Test: 100, 92, 100, 85, 82, 70, 75, 100, 78, 90, 90, 60, 65, 75, 72, 94, 80, 55, 73, 83

_____

2. Survey of favorite pizza toppings: cheese, cheese, cheese, pepperoni, cheese, mushroom, anchovies, cheese, pepperoni, pepperoni

_____

3. Survey of the number of televisions and radios in the home:

student 1: 4, 3	student 5: 4, 2	student 9: 4, 4
student 2: 3, 3	student 6: 4, 1	student 10: 0, 2
student 3: 2, 1	student 7: 4, 2	
student 4: 3, 2	student 8: 5, 5	

_____

4. Fund-raising sales for grade 5: 1,800 boxes of caramels, 600 boxes of mints, 1,000 boxes of white chocolate, 2,000 boxes of dark chocolate

_____

5. Number of raffle tickets sold: Monday, 45; Tuesday, 47; Wednesday, 52; Thursday, 54; Friday, 56; Saturday, 59; Sunday, 60; Monday, 63.

_____

6. Survey classmates on a topic of interest to you. Choose a way to organize your data and present the results to the class.

_____

Review and Remember

Add or subtract.

7.   1,604
     + 808

8.   4,879
     + 3,497

9.   8,888
     − 2,734

10.   3,221
      − 2,622

Multiplication Properties

Find each *n*. Name the property that you used.

1. $6 \times (50 \times 3) = (6 \times n) \times 3$

_____

2. $(n \times 3) \times 15 = 0$

_____

3. $53 \times 1 = n$

_____

4. $4 \times (3 + 2) = (4 \times n) + (4 \times 2)$

_____

5. $n \times (3 + 6) = (4 \times 3) + (4 \times 6)$

_____

6. $(2 \times 8) \times 4 = (n \times 2) \times 4$

_____

Compare. Write $>$, $<$, or $=$.

7. $53 \times 4 \bigcirc 55 \times 6$

8. $1 \times 4 \times 60 \bigcirc 4 \times 60$

9. $64 \times 62 \times 0 \bigcirc 45 \times 25$

Problem Solving

10. Eric buys four cans of dog food for each of his dogs every week. He has two golden retrievers and three German shepherds. Explain what property of multiplication you would use to find out how many cans of dog food Eric buys each week. How many

cans does he buy? _____

11. Write an equation to show how you solved Problem 10. _____

Review and Remember

Compare. Use $>$, $<$, or $=$.

12. $6.03 \bigcirc 6.30$

13. $16.8 + 2 \bigcirc 16.8 + 1.2$

14. $42 - 1.8 \bigcirc 42 - 3.2$

15. $256 \bigcirc 256.0$

16. $1{,}843 \bigcirc 1{,}834$

17. $1.8 \bigcirc 1.0834$

18. $14.03 \bigcirc 14.030$

19. $2.080 \bigcirc 2.80$

20. $16 \times 1 \bigcirc 16 \times 0$

21. $6.09 \bigcirc .609$

22. $47.32 \bigcirc 4.723$

23. $7.609 \bigcirc 7.61$

Problem Solving
Choose the Operation

Answer each question. Explain how you found your answer.

1. How would you find the average score of the basketball teams in a league?

_____

2. The science teacher wants students to work together in groups of 4 to conduct a lab. Each group needs a table with equipment. How can the teacher determine the number of tables he should set up?

_____

3. How many gallons of fuel are needed to fly a plane 1,000 miles?

_____

4. Each seat on a Ferris wheel holds 2 people. Each ride lasts 4 minutes. About how many people can ride the Ferris wheel in one hour?

_____

_____

_____

_____

5. How would you write a number sentence that describes the number of boys and girls in your mathematics class?

_____

6. How would you find how much heavier a 48-lb tuna is than a 26-lb bass?

_____

Review and Remember

Use mental math to solve.

7. $8,000 \times 10 =$ _____ 8. $140 \div 70 =$ _____ 9. $\$45 - \$5.50 =$ _____

10. $600 \times 100 =$ _____ 11. $2,000 \div 50 =$ _____ 12. $\$550 - \$225 =$ _____

Mental Math: Multiplication Patterns Using 10, 100, and 1000

Find each product.

1. $7 \times 100 =$ _____

2. $2{,}000 \times 4 =$ _____

3. $400 \times 400 =$ _____

4. $100 \times 1{,}000 =$ _____

5. $\begin{array}{r} 5{,}000 \\ \times\ \ \ 60 \\ \hline \end{array}$

6. $\begin{array}{r} 3{,}100 \\ \times\ \ \ 40 \\ \hline \end{array}$

7. $\begin{array}{r} 1{,}000 \\ \times\ \ \ 37 \\ \hline \end{array}$

8. $\begin{array}{r} 402{,}000 \\ \times\ \ \ 2{,}000 \\ \hline \end{array}$

Problem Solving

9. Americans buy about 50,000 televisions each day. If the average price of a television is $300, about how much money do Americans spend on televisions each day?

_____

10. Explain how to use mental math to find the product of $50{,}000 \times \$300$.

_____

_____

Review and Remember

Find each n.

11. $6 \times 9 = n$

$n =$ _____

12. $6 \times 7 = n$

$n =$ _____

13. $4 \times 9 = n$

$n =$ _____

14. $7 \times 8 = n$

$n =$ _____

15. $8 \times 3 = n$

$n =$ _____

16. $7 \times 5 = n$

$n =$ _____

17. $8 + 9 = n$

$n =$ _____

18. $7 + 4 = n$

$n =$ _____

19. $7 \times (8 + 1) = n$

$n =$ _____

20. $3 + 8 \times 0 = n$

$n =$ _____

21. $n \times 9 = 81$

$n =$ _____

22. $2 \times (3 + 1) = n$

$n =$ _____

Name _____

Estimating Products

Estimate. Round to the greatest place.

1. 34
    $\times$ 42 _____

2. 568
    $\times$ 43 _____

3. 1,424
    $\times$ 56 _____

4. 413
    $\times$ 452 _____

5. 2,056
    $\times$ 48 _____

6. 835
    $\times$ 36 _____

Problem Solving

7. Mark wants to mount his carved birds on blocks of wood that are 18 inches tall. If Mark has 32 birds, about how many feet of wood will he need to make 32 stands?

_____

_____

8. Mark decides to buy 50 feet of wood. The wood costs $2.99 per foot, and he has $200. Does he have enough money? Explain your answer.

_____

_____

Review and Remember

Find each input or output.

9. Rule: Multiply by 100.

Input	Output
40	
	800
100	
	240,000
	0

10. Rule: Multiply by 400.

Input	Output
200	
	16,000
	2,000,000
1,200	
1,020	

Multiplying by One-Digit Numbers

Estimate each product. Then find the exact answer.

1. $63 \times 2 =$ **2.** $453 \times 3 =$ **3.** $243 \times 2 =$ **4.** $981 \times 9 =$

_____   _____   _____   _____

5.   35
    $\times\ 9$ _____

6.   256
    $\times\ 4$ _____

7.   405
    $\times\ 7$ _____

8.   9,580
    $\times\ 3$ _____

9.   503
    $\times\ 8$ _____

10.   2,085
    $\times\ 2$ _____

Problem Solving

11. Jay, Julio, Juan, and Jake are part of a four-man relay team. At a recent track meet, they each ran 400 meters in about 53 seconds. About how long did it take to complete the relay?

_____

_____

12. Jim ran the 1,600 meter race in four minutes. How does his time compare to the total time run by the relay team?

_____

_____

Review and Remember

Round to the underlined digit.

13. 1\underline{4}.78   **14.** 106.8\underline{3}4   **15.** 1\underline{5}8.26   **16.** 199.9\underline{9}5

_____   _____   _____   _____

17. 4\underline{0}.03   **18.** 1,\underline{4}68,342   **19.** 1.08\underline{3}5   **20.** $15.\underline{6}5

_____   _____   _____   _____

Problem Solving

Guess and Check

Answer each question.

1. Sally took pictures of flowers at the flower show for her photography class. In each of three exhibits, she used one whole roll of film. If she took 48 pictures, how many rolls of 12-exposure and 24-exposure film did she use?

_____

2. A cashier makes change for a $20 bill. If she gives the customer a $10 bill and six other bills, did the cashier change the $20 bill correctly? Explain your answer.

_____

_____

3. Amy earned $30 doing odd jobs for her neighbor. She was paid $10 for raking the yard and the rest for painting the dog house and walking the dog. She earned three times as much for painting the dog house as for walking the dog. How much did she earn for each job?

_____

4. Adam needs $0.95 for the juice machine. He changes a $1 bill and gets 6 coins in return. Does he have the exact change? Explain your answer.

_____

5. Movie tickets for two adults and four children cost $36.00. If adult tickets cost twice as much as children's tickets, how much does each type of ticket cost?

_____

Review and Remember

Use pencil and paper, mental math, or a calculator to solve.

6. $5,205 \div 15 =$ _____   **7.** $152,000 + 5.15 =$ _____   **8.** $63 \times 89 =$ _____

EXPLORE: Understanding Partial Products

Write the partial products for each model. Then write a multiplication sentence.

1.

	20	5
10	10 × 20	10 × 5
3	3 × 20	3 × 5

2.

	200	50	5
50	50 × 200	50 × 50	50 × 5
5	5 × 200	5 × 50	5 × 5

_____   _____

_____   _____

Draw an array to find each product.

3. 65 × 24 = _____

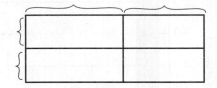

4. 342 × 18 = _____

Problem Solving

5. Mrs. Seiko plans to tile her kitchen floor. Her floor is 15 feet long and 24 feet wide. Each tile is 1 foot by 1 foot. Draw a model of an array to show how many tiles Mrs. Seiko needs.

6. Write an equation for the array in Problem 5.

_____

Review and Remember

Find each product.

7.	**8.**	**9.**	**10.**
23	55	9,824	15,000
× 3	× 4	× 3	× 20

Multiplying by Two-Digit Numbers

Multiply.

1. 45
    × 33

2. 26
    × 19

3. 85
    × 40

4. 19
    × 21

5. 60
    × 24

6. 38
    × 43

7. 98
    × 11

8. 78
    × 87

9. 50
    × 50

10. 88
    × 75

Problem Solving

Use the bar graph for Problems 11–12.

11. If an elephant travels at top speed for one whole day, how far would it travel?

_____

_____

12. How many times faster is a cheetah than a chicken? How many times faster is a cheetah than a rabbit?

_____

_____

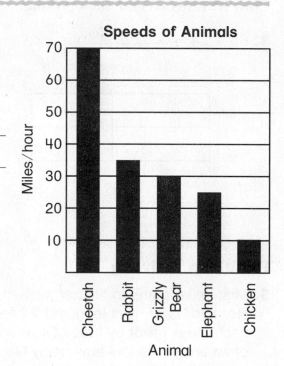

Speeds of Animals

Miles/hour

Cheetah   Rabbit   Grizzly Bear   Elephant   Chicken

Animal

Review and Remember

Compare. Write >, <, or =.

13. 55 × 6 ◯ 154 × 9

14. 50 × 40 ◯ 200

15. 50 × 30 × 0 ◯ 100

16. 22 × 13 ◯ 13 × 22

17. 35 × 20 ◯ 34 × 20

18. 405 × 1 ◯ 450 × 1

19. 106 × 10 ◯ 160 × 10

20. (45 × 2) × 5 ◯ 45 × (2 × 5)

More Multiplying by Two-Digit Numbers

Estimate each product. Then use paper and pencil or a calculator to find the exact answer.

1. $1.45
$\times$ 20 _____

2. 553
$\times$ 25 _____

3. 715
$\times$ 59 _____

4. 243
$\times$ 21 _____

Multiply.

5. $204 \times 89 =$ _____

6. $515 \times 35 =$ _____

7. $802 \times 23 =$ _____

8. $718 \times 99 =$ _____

9. $25 \times 25 =$ _____

10. $1,000 \times 24 =$ _____

11. $315 \times 67 =$ _____

12. $480 \times 63 =$ _____

13. $712 \times 23 =$ _____

Problem Solving

14. Mrs. Seiko is shopping for 360 floor tiles. Store A sells the tiles for $0.79 each. Store B sells the tiles in boxes of 100 tiles for $75.00. Which store offers the best buy? Explain your answer.

_____

_____

15. How much money can Mrs. Seiko save in Problem 11 if she buys the tiles at Store A?

_____

Review and Remember

Find each n. Tell what property is represented in each Problem.

16. $45 \times (3 \times 50) = 45 \times (n \times 3)$

17. $0 \times 18 = n$

18. $1.45 \times (3 \times 5) = (n \times 3) \times 5$

19. $6 \times (4 + 3) = (n \times 4) + (n \times 3)$

20. $18 \times 0 \times 19 = n$

21. $16 \times 15 = n \times 16 \times 15$

Multiplying Greater Numbers

Use pencil and paper or a calculator to find each product.

1.   250
   $\times$ 330

2.   205
   $\times$ 303

3. $4.85
   $\times$ 49

4.   1,437
   $\times$ 348

5.   5,000
   $\times$ 300

6.   5,400
   $\times$ 20

7.   999
   $\times$ 111

8.   20,200
   $\times$ 30

9. 409 $\times$ 23 = _____

10. 268 $\times$ 209 = _____

Problem Solving

11. One of the largest rainbow trout ever caught weighed 42 pounds. If the average restaurant serves 83 pounds of trout in one week, about how many giant rainbow trout would it take to serve 15 restaurants?

_____

12. How many pounds of trout would be needed for an entire year for one restaurant?

_____

Review and Remember

Find each n.

13. $n \div 3 = 24$

$n =$ _____

14. $n \times n = 100$

$n =$ _____

15. $n \times 8 = 0$

$n =$ _____

16. $10 \times 10 = n$

$n =$ _____

17. $20 \div n = 4$

$n =$ _____

18. $40 \times 400 = n$

$n =$ _____

19. $240 \times n = 4,800$

$n =$ _____

20. $50 \times n = 25,000$

$n =$ _____

21. $72 \div n = 12$

$n =$ _____

Problem Solving
Using Money

Answer each question.

1. Anthony has a grocery coupon for $1.00 off one bag of corn chips. If he buys 3 bags for $2.69 each, how much will he pay?

_____

2. Miguel wins 14 tickets at the balloon game. He can redeem the tickets for $0.25 each, or use them to buy a stuffed animal worth $5.75. Which is the best choice? Explain your reasoning.

_____

_____

3. Erin wants to paint her bedroom walls. One gallon of paint costs $15.97; and one quart costs $8.97. She estimates that she needs 6 quarts of paint. What quantities of paint should she buy if she wants to save money? Explain your reasoning.

_____

_____

4. Tim is buying food for a party. He needs 3 pounds of potato salad at $2.69 per pound, 2 pounds of chicken salad at $4.29 per pound, and 1 pound of cheese for $4.69 per pound. He has $20. Does he have enough money to buy the food? Explain your reasoning.

_____

5. Belinda wants to buy favors for 12 guests at her party. Favors come in packages of 5 for $4.95. Can she buy enough favors for all 12 guests for $15.00? Explain.

_____

_____

Review and Remember

Compare. Write >, <, or =.

6. 5.15 $\bigcirc$ 5.05

7. 34.997 $\bigcirc$ 34.797

8. 0.005 $\bigcirc$ 0.05

Relating Multiplication and Division

Write a related multiplication or division sentence. Then find each *n*.

1. $63 \div 7 = n$ **2.** $n \times 9 = 36$ **3.** $7 \times n = 42$

_____ _____ _____

$n =$ _____ $n =$ _____ $n =$ _____

Complete each table.

Rule: Multiply by 4

	Input	Output
4.	7	
5.		24
6.		32

7. Rule: _____

Input	Output
45	9
15	3
25	5

Problem Solving

8. The sun is about 93,000,000 miles from Earth. If a spaceship travels 5,000 miles per hour, explain how you would find the number of days needed to travel to the sun.

_____

_____

_____

9. In 1980, Maxie Anderson and his son crossed North America in a hot-air balloon. They traveled 2,800 miles in 99 hours and 54 minutes. About how far did they travel each hour? Write a multiplication or division sentence to explain your answer.

_____

Review and Remember

Find each answer.

10. $23 \times 15 =$ _____ **11.** $208 \times 64 =$ _____

12. $1,252 \times 49 =$ _____ **13.** $60,000 \times 200 =$ _____

14. $26,800 \times 300 =$ _____ **15.** $402 \times 308 =$ _____

Order of Operations

Solve for *n*.

1. $2 \times 3 + 4 \times 5 = n$

$n = $ _____

2. $8 \times 6 - 2 = n$

$n = $ _____

3. $16 + 4 - 3 + 4 = n$

$n = $ _____

4. $458 \times 0 + 16 \div 4 = n$

$n = $ _____

5. $(8 + 2) \times 3 = n$

$n = $ _____

6. $30 - 2 \times (6 + 4) = n$

$n = $ _____

7. $(3 \times 2) + (4 \times 6) = n$

$n = $ _____

8. $6 + 6 \div 6 - 6 = n$

$n = $ _____

9. $(6 + 6) \div 6 \times 6 - 1 = n$

$n = $ _____

Problem Solving

10. Does the distributive property use order of operations? Explain your answer.

_____

_____

Rewrite each equation. Place parentheses in order to make each equation true.

11. $5 + 5 \times 5 - 5 = 0$ _____

12. $5 + 5 \times 5 - 5 = 45$ _____

13. What letters could you use to help you memorize the correct order of operations? Explain your answer.

_____

Review and Remember

Find each answer.

14. $1.43 + 2.07 = $ _____

15. $43 - 1.89 = $ _____

16. $230 \times 2{,}200 = $ _____

17. $27 \div 3 = $ _____

18. $15 + 1.68 + 0.009 = $ _____

19. $508.3 - 159.639 = $ _____

Mental Math: Patterns in Division

Use a basic fact and patterns to find each quotient.

1. 9)7,200   **2.** 4)360   **3.** 8)48,000

4. 4)2,000   **5.** 7)280   **6.** 3)1,500

7. 2)10,000   **8.** 5)5,000   **9.** 10)1,000

10. 10)3,200   **11.** 5)10,000   **12.** 100)10,000

Problem Solving

13. Explain how compatible numbers are used to mentally divide 24,000 ÷ 6.

_____

_____

14. Compare the two famous bicycle races in the chart at the right. About how many times longer is the Tour de France than the Tour of Somerville? Explain your answer using compatible numbers.

Famous Bicycle Races	
Name	Distance in Miles
Tour de France	2,500–3,000
Tour of Somerville	50

_____

Review and Remember

Estimate each product.

15. 6,356 × 57 = _____   **16.** 508 × 35 = _____

17. 989 × 96 = _____   **18.** 423 × 456 = _____

19. 6,000 × 25 = _____   **20.** 58 × 63 = _____

Estimating Quotients of Whole Numbers

Estimate each quotient using compatible numbers. Tell what compatible numbers you used.

1. 6)1,720   **2.** 8)4,948   **3.** 4)19,660   **4.** 6)54,731

_____   _____   _____   _____

5. 6)29,437   **6.** 9)6,400   **7.** 8)3,362   **8.** 3)128

_____   _____   _____   _____

9. 7)3,473   **10.** 4)3,517   **11.** 2)163   **12.** 9)8,257

_____   _____   _____   _____

Problem Solving

13. The Great Wall of China is 3,950 miles long. If you walked without stopping at four miles per hour, could you walk the length of the Great Wall in one month? Use estimation to explain your answer.

_____

14. Using the information in Problem 13, about how many days would it take to walk the length of the Great Wall?

_____

Review and Remember

Solve. Tell what method you used.

15. $48.2 \times 7 =$ _____   **16.** $4,000 \div 5 =$ _____

17. $7.6534 - 4.873 =$ _____   **18.** $3,600 - 1,600 =$ _____

19. $1.58 + 6 + 3.42 + 1.2 =$ _____   **20.** $2.489 - 1.236 =$ _____

21. 76.3   **22.** 35.331   **23.** 5.002
     $\times\ \ \ 4$ $+\ \ 1.8$ $\times\ \ \ 3$

Divisibility Rules

Tell if each number is divisible by 2, 3, 4, 5, 6, 9, or 10.

1. 1,422

2. 1,065,330

3. 3,332

4. 12,345

_____   _____   _____   _____

5. 72,921

6. 50,520

7. 321,321

8. 5,451

_____   _____   _____   _____

9. 1,234

10. 6,660

11. 1,422

12. 3,781

_____   _____   _____   _____

Problem Solving

13. Sally is trying to think of a number that is divisible by 9 but not divisible by 3. Can you help her? Explain.

_____

14. Write a divisibility rule for each number.

Number	Rule
2	
3	
4	
5	
6	
9	
10	

Review and Remember

Find each n.

15. $6 \times n = 6$

$n =$ _____

16. $5 \times n = 0$

$n =$ _____

17. $15 \times 3 = n \times 15$

$n =$ _____

18. $6,000 \div n = 3,000$

$n =$ _____

19. $8 \times (2 + 3) = (n \times 2) + (n \times 3)$

$n =$ _____

Problem Solving
Interpreting Remainders

Answer each question. Give a reason for your choice.

Teams are being set for the school volleyball tournament. The players include 38 students, 4 teachers, the principal, the librarian, the nurse, and 8 parents. Each team must have the same number of adults.

1. How many adults are playing?

   a. 88 adults

   b. 12 adults

   c. 15 adults

2. Which divisibility rule is used to find the greatest possible number of teams with the same number of adults?

   a. divisibility by 2

   b. divisibility by 3

   c. divisibility by 4

3. What is the greatest possible number of teams?

   a. 3 teams

   b. 4 teams

   c. 5 teams

4. What number sentence could be used to find the greatest number of students on each team?

   a. $38 \div 5 = 7 \text{ R3}$

   b. $38 \div 3 = 12 \text{ R2}$

   c. $38 \times 5 = 440$

5. How many teams will have one extra player each? How do you know?

_____

Review and Remember

Solve.

6. $25.35 - $5.25 = _____

7. $1,342 - $1,102.50 = _____

8. $132 × 5 = _____

9. $500 ÷ 10 = _____

10. $1,000 + $250 + $500 = _____

11. $650 + $250 ÷ 5 = _____

Dividing by One-Digit Divisors

Divide.

1. 5)408   **2.** 3)265   **3.** 4)783   **4.** 9)463

5. 6)90   **6.** 5)565   **7.** 7)434   **8.** 2)3,389

9. 5)135   **10.** 4)307   **11.** 8)728   **12.** 4)12,459

Problem Solving

13. Fifth-grade students raised $580.50 for charity. They plan to donate the money to three separate charities. Can they give $200 to each charity?

_____

14. The school is planning to hold a field day next Saturday for 350 students. Each student will be given a frozen yogurt. If frozen yogurts come in boxes of 6 or 4, how many boxes does the school need to buy in order to have exactly the correct amount?

_____

Review and Remember

Complete each table.

Rule: Multiply by 25

	Input	Output
15.	15	
16.		100
17.	30	

18. Rule: _____

	Input	Output
	480	96
19.	365	
20.		101

Short Division

Use short division to find each quotient. Check Problems 1–4 by multiplying.

1. 8)95   **2.** 6)205   **3.** 4)970   **4.** 5)635

5. 7)4,146   **6.** 2)337   **7.** 9)5,514   **8.** 4)85,381

9. 5)257   **10.** 9)768   **11.** 2)2,468   **12.** 3)6,981

Problem Solving

13. There are 651 students at Golden Hill School. If the school has three lunch periods, can the same number of students attend each lunch? Explain your answer using one of the rules of divisibility.

_____

14. Students at Golden Hill School enjoy pizza for lunch. Each pizza is cut into eight slices. If every student has two slices, how many pizzas are served?

_____

Review and Remember

Find each product.

15. $403 \times 4 =$ _____   **16.** $6,008 \times 5 =$ _____

17. $90,801 \times 8 =$ _____   **18.** $9,030 \times 7 =$ _____

19. $509 \times 3 =$ _____   **20.** $606 \times 6 =$ _____

Zeros in the Quotient

Divide. Check by multiplying.

1. $3\overline{)2,106}$ **2.** $2\overline{)4,813}$ **3.** $4\overline{)12,813}$ **4.** $7\overline{)7,014}$

5. $6\overline{)865}$ **6.** $5\overline{)6,501}$ **7.** $8\overline{)3,608}$ **8.** $6\overline{)9,012}$

9. $7\overline{)843}$ **10.** $3\overline{)521}$ **11.** $3\overline{)909}$ **12.** $5\overline{)1,500}$

Problem Solving

13. Food for the fifth-grade picnic costs $316. The bus to the picnic costs $100. If the costs are being shared equally by four classes, how much will each class pay?

_____

14. Mrs. Clay ordered 240 hot dogs for the 90 students going to the picnic. How many hot dogs can each student eat? Can some eat more than others? Explain your answer.

_____

Review and Remember

Solve for *n*. Use order of operations.

15. $5 + 12 \div 4 = n$ **16.** $3 \times (4 + 2) = n$ **17.** $42 \div 6 + 3 \times 2 = n$

n = _____   n = _____   n = _____

18. $15 + 20 \div 4 - 2 = n$ **19.** $6 \times 3 - 5 + 3 = n$ **20.** $20 - 2 \times (5 + 2) = n$

n = _____   n = _____   n = _____

Problem Solving
Work Backwards

Work backwards to solve Problems 1–6.

1. The volleyball tournament expenses totaled $1,125. It cost $850 for refreshments and $25 for a custodian. The rest was used to pay two referees. How much did each referee get paid?

   _____

2. Mrs. Joyce arrived home from her errands with $50 left in her wallet. She had spent $85 on groceries, $10 at the cleaners, and $6.80 at the Post Office. How much money did she have before she went on the errands?

   _____

3. What number am I? If you divide me by 7, subtract 5, and multiply by 9, the

   result is 27. _____

4. It cost Mr. and Mrs. Parker $99 to take their two children to a baseball game. Each person had 2 hot dogs at $2.50 each and a large soda at $1.25 each. It cost $10 for parking. How much did each ticket cost?

   _____

5. Chris gets a $6 weekly allowance. His brother gets twice as much. If Chris's mother gives her children a total of $27, how much does she

   give her daughter? _____

6. Mrs. Fox runs a car pool. She drives 3 blocks north to pick up Amy, 5 blocks west to pick up Sheila, two blocks north to pick up Julie, 16 blocks east to pick up Melissa, and then 5 blocks south to school. How far is

   the school from her home? _____

Review and Remember

Find the answer.

7. $500 \div 5 =$ _____

8. $1,600 \div 10 =$ _____

9. $320 \div 8 =$ _____

10. $333 \div 3 =$ _____

11. $241 \div 2 =$ _____

12. $633 \div 3 =$ _____

13. $2,438 \div 6 =$ _____

14. $368 \div 5 =$ _____

15. $784 \div 7 =$ _____

EXPLORE: Finding Averages

Find the mean of each set of data.

1. 23, 5, 9, 19, 9 _____

2. 78, 83, 75, 92 _____

3. 538, 266 _____

4. 30, 40, 50 _____

5. 253, 200, 300 _____

6. 1,021; 598; 634; 258; 34 _____

7. 135, 258, 0 _____

8. 78, 100, 50 _____

9. $58, $35, $26, $57 _____

Problem Solving

10. Use the table at the right to answer the questions. What is the mean of Alex's quiz grades? What is the median of his quiz grades? Would the mean or the median be the best representation of his grades? Explain your answer.

_____

_____

11. Create your own word problem to practice finding averages. Share your problem with a classmate.

_____

Alex's Quiz Grades	
Quiz	Grade
1	78
2	78
3	80
4	0
5	50
6	79
7	83

Review and Remember

Use the following set of numbers for Problems 12–14.

32   28   19   41   57   112   32   44   35

12. Find the median. _____

13. Find the mode. _____

14. Find the range. _____

Use the following set of numbers for Problems 15–17.

$17,000 $9,000 $16,000 $9,000 $8,000

15. Find the median. _____

16. Find the mode. _____

17. Find the range. _____

Dividing With Greater Dividends

Divide.

1. 3)89,341   **2.** 2)40,006   **3.** 4)$61,804   **4.** 8)72,183

5. 7)21,014   **6.** 6)33,077   **7.** 8)$24,032   **8.** 5)52,462

9. 3)7,805   **10.** 5)$50,535   **11.** 8)63,943   **12.** 9)18,456

Problem Solving

13. There are 2,890 passengers on the Queen Elizabeth II. How many tables would you need if you seat eight passengers at each table for dinner? Write a division sentence to explain your answer.

_____

14. The Queen Elizabeth II sailed 4,668 miles in 8 days. Did the ship average more than 500 miles per day? Write a multiplication or division sentence to explain your answer.

_____

Review and Remember

Solve.

15. 6,123.42
       −   68.025

16.   253
        × 28

17.   8.1893
        + 4.986

18. 65
        3.48
       + 0.009

19. 43
       − 0.814

20. 7)738

Problem Solving

Mean, Median, and Mode

Use the table below to solve Problems 1–5.

1. Should the bowling league use the
mean, median, or mode to determine
the average score of the team?
Explain.

_____

_____

_____

Bowling Scores					
Game	Pedro	John	Pam	Brian	Lisa
1	75	73	85	68	75
2	82	110	80	75	78
3	73	74	75	75	78
4	75	73	80	42	82
5	75	70	75	70	75

2. Find the mean score for John's five
games of bowling. How does this
compare to the median and mode?

_____

_____

3. If John had scored 100 for his second game, how would this have affected
the mean, median, and mode for his scores?

_____

_____

4. Would you use mean, median, or mode to describe Brian's data? Explain.

_____

5. Create a problem of your own using the mean of one or more of the
students' bowling scores.

_____

_____

Review and Remember

Compare. Use >, <, or =.

6. 635 ◯ 653   **7.** 25.8 ◯ 2.58   **8.** $25 ◯ $25.00   **9.** 67.3 ◯ 67.8

10. 403.6 ◯ 430.06   **11.** 36.4 ◯ 36.400   **12.** 1.002 ◯ 1.02

Mental Math: Patterns in Division

Use mental math to find each quotient. Check by multiplying.

1. $40\overline{)160}$ **2.** $300\overline{)2,400}$ **3.** $90\overline{)900}$

4. $80\overline{)480}$ **5.** $7\overline{)700}$ **6.** $7\overline{)4,900}$

Find each *n*.

7. $50 \times n = 2,500$ **8.** $20 \times n = 20$ **9.** $n \times 60 = 3,600$

    $n =$ _____ $n =$ _____ $n =$ _____

10. $n \times 90 = 900$ **11.** $n \times 1,000 = 6,000$ **12.** $30 \times n = 3,000$

    $n =$ _____ $n =$ _____ $n =$ _____

Problem Solving

13. During Cinco de Mayo, 30 fifth graders danced for a total of 270 hours. How many hours did each fifth grader dance?

_____

14. There are 692 students at Drago Elementary School. If each student dances 9 hours during Cinco de Mayo, how many hours will they have danced?

_____

Review and Remember

Find each quotient.

15. $4,931 \div 7$ **16.** $232 \div 6$ **17.** $6,483 \div 9$

18. $5,000 \div 5$ **19.** $24,731 \div 8$ **20.** $16,002 \div 2$

21. $4,408 \div 4$ **22.** $1,005 \div 3$ **23.** $811 \div 10$

Estimating Quotients

Use compatible numbers to estimate each quotient.

1. 79)165

2. 81)550

3. 37)2,783

4. 62)3,548

5. 52)36,894

6. 97)8,964

7. 18)4,162

8. 71)64,893

9. 19)12,002

Problem Solving

10. It took Michael about 3 weeks to read a 400-page book. About how many pages did he read each day? Explain your answer.

_____

_____

_____

_____

11. Michael read the four books listed in the chart at the right. What was the average number of pages in these four books?

_____

Title	Pages per Book
Frankenstein	349
Journey to the Center of the Earth	316
Hound of the Baskervilles	245
The Call of the Wild	102

Review and Remember

Solve.

12. 234
  46
 + 38

13. 6,003
 − 4,598

14. 256
 × 12

15. 568 ÷ 2 = _____

16. 68 + 3.2 + 2 = _____

17. $4,030 × 20 = _____

Problem Solving
Reasonable Answers

Read the paragraph and answer each question.

The baseball team at Johnson School needs new uniforms. There are 25 players on the team. Each player is going to get a uniform that consists of a shirt, a pair of pants, and a cap.

1. Shirts come in packages of 7. How many packages should the team order?

_____

2. Baseball caps come in packages of 6. Would it be reasonable to order 25 packages? Explain.

_____

3. The team has $100 to spend on shirts. If the price of a package of 7 shirts is $20, will the team be able to pay for all of the shirts? Explain.

_____

4. The price of one pair of pants is $5, and the price of a package of 5 pairs of pants is $20. The pitcher, Joe, thinks that it is a better deal to buy 5 packages of five pants than to buy the pants individually. Is what Joe says reasonable?

_____

Review and Remember

Round each to the nearest tenth.

5. 8.79 _____   **6.** 3.32 _____   **7.** 14.57 _____   **8.** 218.98 _____

Round each to the nearest one.

9. 7.62 _____   **10.** 110.88 _____   **11.** 16.29 _____   **12.** 1,000.78 _____

Dividing by Two-Digit Divisors

Estimate each quotient. Then divide.

1. 28)126   **2.** 32)239   **3.** 66)239   **4.** 48)356

5. 17)89   **6.** 63)536   **7.** 56)438   **8.** 35)168

Problem Solving

9. Mrs. Ray's class collected 789 soda cans to be recycled. Cans are packed in cartons with 24 cans per carton. How many cartons does Mrs. Ray's class fill?

_____

10. Mrs. Griffith's class packed 45 cartons with 24 soda cans per carton. How many more cans did Mrs. Griffith's class collect than Mrs. Ray's class?

_____

11. The fifth grade class packed a total of 352 cartons. There are 7 fifth grade classes. About how many cartons did each class pack?

_____

12. By crushing the cans, Mr. Anderson's class fits twice as many cans in each carton. They recycle 960 cans. How many cartons do they need?

_____

Review and Remember

Find each answer. Use order of operations.

13. $16 + 3 \times 5 - 7 =$ _____   **14.** $(16 + 2) \times (15 + 5) =$ _____

15. $16 \div 4 + 8 \times 0 =$ _____   **16.** $238 + 1 \times 62 =$ _____

17. $6 \times 3 - 4 + 2 =$ _____   **18.** $20 - 10 + 6 - 5 =$ _____

19. $2 \times (4 + 5) =$ _____   **20.** $4 + 5 \times 2 - 7 =$ _____

EXPLORE: Two-Digit Quotients

Use base-ten blocks to divide.

1. 15)345   **2.** 12)135   **3.** 21)319   **4.** 19)209

5. 18)378   **6.** 24)219   **7.** 11)349   **8.** 22)220

Problem Solving

Use the table at the right to answer
Problems 9–10.

9. About how many pounds of plastic
is collected for recycling per day?
Per year?

_____

_____

Monthly Recycling Rates	
Item	**Pounds Collected**
Newspaper	298,460
Aluminum	400
Glass	1,636
Plastic	960

10. Estimate the number of pounds
of newspaper collected per day.
Per year.

_____

_____

Review and Remember

Tell which numbers are divisible by 2, 3, 4, 5, 6, 9, and 10.

11. 2,225   **12.** 84,000   **13.** 3,100   **14.** 9,486

_____   _____   _____   _____

_____   _____   _____   _____

15. 7,380   **16.** 7,423   **17.** 450   **18.** 112

_____   _____   _____   _____

Two-Digit Quotients

Divide and check.

1. 36)856

2. 84)653

3. 91)3,648

4. 17)863

5. 64)854

6. 55)660

7. 24)252

8. 49)3,970

9. 13)396

Problem Solving

10. Mr. Cordero drives from Phoenix to Flagstaff. If he drives 136 miles at 65 miles per hour, about how long does the trip take?

_____

11. From Flagstaff, Mr. Cordero plans to drive 329 miles to Albuquerque and another 290 miles to Amarillo. Can he make the whole trip from Phoenix to Amarillo in two days? Explain your answer.

_____

_____

_____

Review and Remember

Solve.

12. $106 \times 13 =$ _____

13. $2,683 \div 3 =$ _____

14. $482 + 18 =$ _____

15. $100 \times 100 =$ _____

16. $348 - 129 =$ _____

17. $4,800 \div 60 =$ _____

18. $4 \times 350 =$ _____

19. $500 \div 25 =$ _____

20. $8 \times (7 + 6) =$ _____

Problem Solving
Make a Table

Organize the following information in a table. Use the table to solve Problems 1–4.

Mrs. Santiago is inviting 12 children to her son's birthday party. She plans to serve each child 2 slices of pizza, 2 cans of juice, and one slice of carrot cake. An 8-slice pizza costs $6.00, a six-pack of juice costs $2.99, and a large carrot cake costs $9.99. Each guest will also receive a $5.00 toy. Mrs. Santiago spent $13.00 on paper plates, napkins, and plastic forks.

1. How much will Mrs. Santiago spend on food?_____

2. How much will she spend all together?_____

3. How could Mrs. Santiago reduce her party expenses by about one half?

_____

4. How much would the party cost if Mrs. Santiago decides not to buy a toy for each guest?

_____

Review and Remember

	Rule: Multiply by 3	
	Input	Output
5.	$13.85	
6.		$20.10
7.		$111
8.	$20.55	

	Rule: Divide by 2	
	Input	Output
9.	102	
10.		32 R1
11.		45
12.	412	

Dividing Greater Numbers

Find each quotient.

1. 25)3,087   **2.** 33)6,020   **3.** 42)4,370

4. 60)3,660   **5.** 79)16,037   **6.** 56)1,280

7. 63)27,450   **8.** 17)2,987   **9.** 12)2,444

Problem Solving

Use the table at the right to solve
Problems 10–12.

10. During the concert tour, sales of tickets
to students totaled $331,125. How many
students attended the concerts?

_____

11. Twelve-year-old Juanita will be attending
the concert with her younger brother,
her parents, and her elderly grandmother.
How much will the family pay for their tickets?

_____

12. Hillside School bought $325 worth of student
tickets. How many students are going to the concert?

_____

Concert Tickets	
Adults	$37
Students (12 yrs–18 yrs)	$25
Children (under 12 yrs)	$15
Senior Citizens	$15

Review and Remember

Solve.

13. 36.4 + 28.32 + 24.6   **14.** 76.4 − 23.82   **15.** 243 − 151

_____

16. $8.47 + $16.50 + $15   **17.** 238 − 46.003   **18.** 14,247 + 3,843 + 929

_____

Problem Solving
Using Operations

Choose a method. Use paper and pencil or a calculator to solve
Problems 1–5.

1. Mrs. Barnes has invited 165 people to an anniversary party.
She plans to seat 10 people per table. How many tables will she
have to set up?

_____

2. The centerpiece for each table will be a vase with 8 red carnations.
How many dozen carnations will she have to order?

_____

3. Mrs. Barnes is ordering cold cuts for 165 people. If each platter
serves up to 75 people, how many platters will she order?

_____

4. Mrs. Barnes is decorating each of three entrances to the hall with
balloons. Each entrance will have 6 plain balloons and 2 special
balloons. Plain balloons cost $0.50 each and special balloons cost
twice as much. How much will she spend on balloons?

_____

5. The party is starting promptly at 7 P.M. On her way to the hall
Mrs. Barnes needs 45 minutes to pick up the cold cuts, flowers, and
balloons. She also needs about 1 hour and 10 minutes to decorate
the hall. What time should she leave home for the party?

_____

Review and Remember

Find each n.

6. $n \times n = 144$

$n =$ _____

7. $n + 65 = 65 + 30$

$n =$ _____

8. $1,500 \div n = 30$

$n =$ _____

9. $2,400 \div 200 = n$

$n =$ _____

10. $n \times 340 = 340$

$n =$ _____

11. $65 \times n = 0$

$n =$ _____

Geometric Ideas

Draw an example of each of the following. Label your drawings.

1. point *C*   **2.** line *AB*   **3.** ray *AB*   **4.** line segment *AB*

Use the drawing at the right to answer Problems 5–11.
Use letters and symbols.

5. Name two parallel lines. _____

6. Name the line perpendicular to line *GH*. _____

7. What point lies on line *ED*? _____

8. What kind of lines are *ED* and *FD*? _____

9. What kind of lines are *EF* and *FD*? _____

10. Name a ray on line *ED*. _____

11. What do points *E*, *F*, and *H* name? _____

Problem Solving

12. Describe something in your classroom that illustrates a line, a line segment, a ray,

intersecting lines, and parallel lines. _____

_____

13. A parking lot is 180 feet wide. A crew paints three white lines to divide the lot into
equal lanes. How wide is each lane? Draw a diagram to illustrate your answer.

_____

Review and Remember

Find each answer using Mental Math.

14. $354 \times 1,000 =$ _____   **15.** $268 + 32 + 59 =$ _____

16. $540,000 \div 9 =$ _____   **17.** $500 - 200 =$ _____

EXPLORE: Classifying Angles

Classify each angle as right, straight, acute, or obtuse.

1.

2.

3.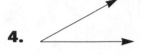

_____   _____   _____   _____

Use the drawing at the right to answer Problems 5–8.

5. Name an acute angle. _____

6. Name a right angle. _____

7. Name a straight angle. _____

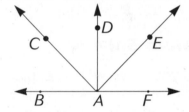

8. What can you say about AD and BF? _____

Problem Solving

9. Describe something in your home that illustrates a right angle, an acute angle, and an

obtuse angle. _____

_____

10. Write a short paragraph to describe different times when the hands of a clock

illustrate examples of different kinds of angles. _____

_____

Review and Remember

Solve.

11. $(16 \times 2) + (3 \times 6) =$ _____

12. $(8 \times 2) + (8 \times 5) =$ _____

13. $5 + 16 \div 4 - 1 =$ _____

14. $58 \times 35 \times 0 \times 16 =$ _____

15. $45 \div 9 \times 1 \div 5 =$ _____

16. $5 \times 3 - 4 \times 3 =$ _____

Use with Grade 5, text pages 250-251.

Working With Angles

Measure each angle with a protractor.

1.

2.

3.

4.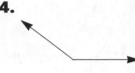

_____   _____   _____   _____

Use a protractor to draw each angle.

5. 35°   **6.** 180°   **7.** 145°   **8.** 18°

Problem Solving

9. In your own words, explain how to use a protractor to measure an angle.

_____

_____

_____

_____

_____

10. Draw three triangles with different shapes. Measure the three angles inside each triangle. What is the sum of the angles of each triangle? Write a conclusion to describe your results.

_____

_____

Review and Remember

Solve using front-end estimation.

11. $6,528 \div 8 =$ _____   **12.** $49,382 \div 6 =$ _____   **13.** $39,843 \div 9 =$ _____

14. $2,682 \div 5 =$ _____   **15.** $29,483 \div 3 =$ _____   **16.** $438,296 \div 8 =$ _____

Polygons

Draw an example of each polygon.

1. triangle   **2.** quadrilateral   **3.** octagon   **4.** hexagon

Name each polygon shown below.

5. _____   **6.** _____   **7.** _____   **8.** _____

Use the drawing at the right to name an example of each of the following geometric figures.

9. a triangle   **10.** a quadrilateral

_____   _____

11. a pentagon   **12.** perpendicular line segments

_____   _____

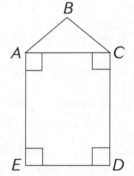

Problem Solving

13. On a separate sheet of paper, draw a simple quilt pattern that is made up of triangles.

14. Draw another quilt pattern that includes at least three different types of polygons.

Review and Remember

Find the mean, range, mode, and median of each of the following sets of numbers.

15. 25, 38, 46, 45, 11   **16.** $1,100, $1,000, $1,000, $7,500

_____   _____

Problem Solving
Spatial Reasoning

Use the drawing of a tablecloth design to answer the following questions.

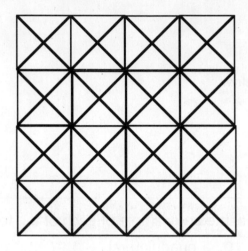

1. How many of the smallest squares are in the tablecloth? _____

2. How many of the smallest triangles are in the tablecloth? _____

3. If another row was added to the tablecloth, how many of
the smallest triangles would be added? _____

4. If the tablecloth is folded in half, and then folded in half
again, how many of the smallest triangles would be showing? _____

Review and Remember

Find each answer.

5. $16 - 9 =$ _____

6. $3 \times 7 =$ _____

7. $5 \times 9 =$ _____

8. $8 + 7 =$ _____

Classifying Triangles

Classify each triangle by its angles and sides.

1.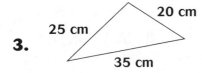

2.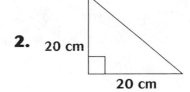

_____

3.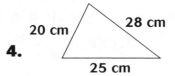

4.

_____

Use the drawing at the right to name an example
of each of the following figures.

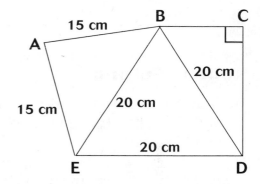

5. right triangle _____

6. equilateral triangle _____

7. obtuse isosceles triangle _____

8. right angle _____

Problem Solving

9. Mr. Rosario's backyard is shaped like a quadrilateral.
Each side is 30 feet. He wants to put plants along three
sides of the yard. If they are three feet apart, how many
bushes will he need?

_____ Draw a diagram to explain.

Review and Remember

Solve using mental math.

10. $110 \times 2 =$ _____ **11** $99 \times 4 =$ _____ **12.** $180 \div 3 =$ _____

13. $(180 - 100) \div 2 =$ ___ **14.** $(156 - 6) \div 3 =$ ___ **15.** $(180 - 120) \div 2 =$ ___

EXPLORE: The Sum of the Angles of a Triangle

Find each unknown angle. Measure to check your answer.

1.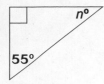

2.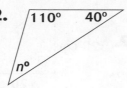

3.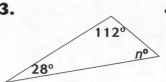

4.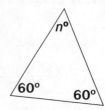

n = _____   n = _____   n = _____   n = _____

Could each of these sets of angles form a triangle? Write yes or no. Explain your answer.

5. $48°$, $16°$, $116°$ **6.** $30°$, $60°$, $90°$ **7.** $90°$, $90°$, $0°$ **8.** $59°$, $59°$, $59°$

_____   _____   _____   _____

_____   _____   _____   _____

_____   _____   _____   _____

Problem Solving

9. Draw three different-sized equilateral triangles. Make a prediction about the measure of their angles. Use a protractor to check your prediction. Was your prediction correct? Explain.

_____

_____

10. Draw three different-sized isosceles triangles. Make a prediction about the measure of their angles. Use a protractor to check your prediction. Was your prediction correct? Explain.

_____

_____

Review and Remember

Compare. Use >, <, or =.

11. $432 \div 2$ ◯ $532 \div 2$ **12.** $3,200 \times 40$ ◯ $30,000 \times 60$

13. $8 \times (4 + 2)$ ◯ $(8 \times 4) + (8 \times 2)$ **14.** 200×200 ◯ $20 \times 2,000$

Classifying Quadrilaterals

Use the figures at the right to answer Problems 1–5.

1. Which are polygons? _____

2. Which are rectangles? _____

3. Which are parallelograms? _____

4. Which are rhombuses? _____

5. Which are trapezoids? _____

Problem Solving

6. What type of quadrilateral can be formed using two equilateral triangles?

_____

7. Lindsay has a piece of construction paper 12 inches by 14 inches. She mounts a picture on the construction paper leaving a 2-inch border around the picture. What shape is the picture? What size is the picture? Make a drawing to illustrate your answer.

_____

Review and Remember

Place the numbers 1–9 in the empty boxes so that each row and column completes a mathematical equation.

	×		÷		= 27
−		÷		+	
	−		+		= 11
+		+		+	
	+		+		= 15
= 12		= 9		= 15	

Problem Solving
Find a Pattern

Draw the next figure in each pattern.

1.   _____

2.   _____

3.   _____

Continue the pattern.

4. 1, 2, 4, 7, _____, _____, _____   **5.** 1, 2, 4, 8, 16, _____, _____, _____

6. Sandra's garden is in the shape of an octagon. Make a drawing to show one line of symmetry she would use to divide her garden into two equal areas.

Review and Remember

Divide.

7. 40)248   **8.** 70)520   **9.** 60)335   **10.** 42)384

11. 78)470   **12.** 39)209   **13.** 93)705   **14.** 63)468

Congruent Figures and Transformations

Tell how each figure was moved. Write *slide*, *flip*, or *turn*.

1.

_____

2.

_____

3.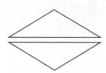

_____

4.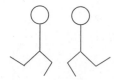

_____

5.

_____

6.

_____

Tell if each pair of figures is congruent. Write yes or no.

7.

_____

8.

_____

9.

_____

10.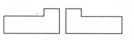

_____

Problem Solving

11. Think about the letters of the alphabet, both capital and lower case. Which letters can be turned, flipped, or both to produce a letter?

_____

12. Draw your own examples of figures that show a slide, a flip, and a turn.

Review and Remember

Use short division to find each answer.

13. $3{,}408 \div 2 =$ _____

14. $60{,}183 \div 6 =$ _____

15. $5{,}632 \div 7 =$ _____

16. $64{,}000 \div 8 =$ _____

Looking at Similar Figures

Tell if the shapes in each pair are similar. Write *yes* or *no*.

1.    **2.**    **3.** 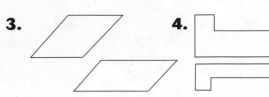   **4.**

_____   _____   _____   _____

5. Draw similar pentagons.

6. Draw a shape similar to the one at the right.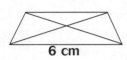
6 cm

7. Imagine an isosceles triangle with sides measuring 6 cm, 6 cm, and 5 cm. What are some possible measurements of similar triangles?

_____

Problem Solving

8. Juana bought a wallpaper border for her bedroom. Her room measures 8 feet by 10 feet. The border costs 59 cents per foot. How much did she pay for the border?

_____

9. Juana's father likes the wallpaper border and asks her to buy a border for the family room. The family room is exactly twice as large as Juana's bedroom. How much will

she pay for this border? Use Mental Math. _____

Review and Remember

Find each answer.

10. $8\overline{)5,387}$ **11.** $\begin{array}{r} 315 \\ \times\ 209 \\ \hline \end{array}$ **12.** $\begin{array}{r} 16 \\ -\ 2.038 \\ \hline \end{array}$ **13.** $\begin{array}{r} 168 \\ 2.3 \\ +\ 0.09 \\ \hline \end{array}$

Problem Solving
Using Symmetry

Half of each design is missing. Each dashed line is a line of symmetry.
Trace the design and draw the other half.

1.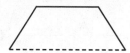

2.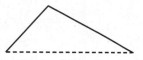

3.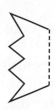

4.

5.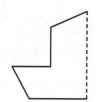

6.

Look at each drawing. Draw in at least one line of symmetry.

7.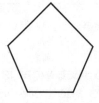

8.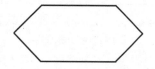

9.

Review and Remember

Use the drawing at the right to answer Exercises 10–16.

10. Name two parallel lines. _____

11. Name two perpendicular lines. _____

12. What point lies on line AC ? _____

13. Name six line segments. _____

14. What kind of lines are AE and AC? _____

15. Name a ray on AE. _____

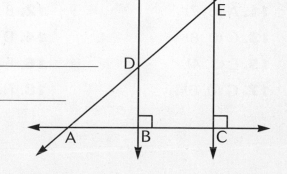

EXPLORE: Circles

Use the circle at the right to answer Problems 1–5.

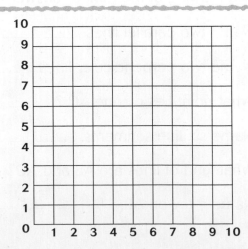

1. Name a radius. _____

2. Name a diameter. _____

3. Name the center. _____

4. Name a chord. _____

5. Name the longest chord. _____

6. If the radius of a circle is 7 cm, what is the diameter? _____

7. If the diameter of a circle is 10 cm, what is the radius? _____

8. Can a radius also be a chord? _____

_____

Problem Solving

9. Brianne has a circular swimming pool. If the radius of the pool is 15 feet, what is the longest straight distance she can swim from one edge of the pool to another?

_____

10. Imagine that you shape a piece of string to form an octagon. Each side of the octagon is 8 inches. How long is the string?

_____

Review and Remember

Graph each ordered pair.

11. A (6, 7)   **12.** B (7, 0)

13. C (0, 8)   **14.** D (4, 3)

15. E (3, 4)   **16.** F (1, 9)

17. G (0, 0)   **18.** H (9, 9)

Solid Figures

Identify these geometric space figures from each pattern.

1.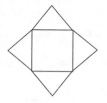

2.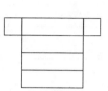

3.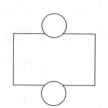

4.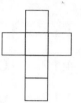

_____   _____   _____   _____

Identify these figures.

5.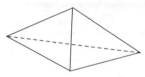

6.

7.

8.

_____   _____   _____   _____

Problem Solving

9. What do you predict an octagonal prism looks like? Try to draw an

example. _____

10. The fifth-grade class is ordering several 9-inch pizzas. What is the
size and shape of the smallest box that one of these pizzas can be

delivered in? _____

_____

Review and Remember

Name each ordered pair from the graph.

11. A _____

12. B _____

13. C _____

14. D _____

15. E _____

16. F _____

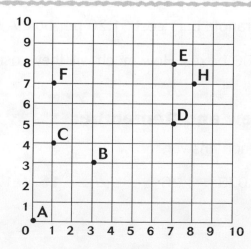

Multiplying Decimals by 10, 100, and 1,000

Use patterns to find each product.

1. $4.12 \times 1 =$ _____

$4.12 \times 10 =$ _____

$4.12 \times 100 =$ _____

$4.12 \times 1,000 =$ _____

2. $0.0023 \times 1 =$ _____

$0.0023 \times 10 =$ _____

$0.0023 \times 100 =$ _____

$0.0023 \times 1,000 =$ _____

3. $67.9 \times 1 =$ _____

$67.9 \times 10 =$ _____

$67.9 \times 100 =$ _____

$67.9 \times 1,000 =$ _____

Follow the rule to find each output.

Rule: Multiply by 100

	Input	Output
4.	2.3	
5.	12.5	
6.	0.12	

Rule: Multiply by 1,000

	Input	Output
7.	0.163	
8.	5.23	
9.	9.27	

Find each *n*.

10. $0.298 \times n = 2.98$

$n =$ _____

11. $9.078 \times n = 9,078$

$n =$ _____

12. $n \times 1 = 1.209$

$n =$ _____

Problem Solving

13. Timothy bikes 1.7 miles to school and 1.7 miles home each day.

How many miles does he bike in 10 days? _____

14. Granola bars cost $1.20 per box. A summer camp has ordered

100 boxes. How much will they cost altogether? _____

Review and Remember

Find each answer.

15. $0.023 + 1.26 =$ _____

16. $9.12 - 0.36 =$ _____

17. $10 + 0.25 =$ _____

Multiplying Decimals by Whole Numbers

Find each product.

1. 5.46
   $\times\ \ \ 3$

2. 11.23
   $\times\ \ \ \ 5$

3. 0.013
   $\times\ \ \ \ 6$

4. 2.98
   $\times\ \ 14$

5. 0.123
   $\times\ \ 29$

6. 0.002
   $\times\ \ 12$

7. 7.962
   $\times\ \ \ \ 8$

8. 52.36
   $\times\ \ 62$

9. $8 \times 123.5 =$ _____

10. $17 \times 90.21 =$ _____

11. $8.093 \times 5 =$ _____

12. $12 \times 5.0013 =$ _____

Problem Solving

13. If one carton of oil costs $23.97, how much do one dozen cartons

cost? _____

14. Greg is buying six notebooks for school. Each costs $1.69. How

much change will he get from $20.00? _____

Review and Remember

Find each n. Name the property used.

15. $56 \times n = 43 \times 56$

$n =$ _____

16. $8 \times (n \times 4) = (8 \times 3) \times 4$

$n =$ _____

Estimating the Product of a Whole Number and a Decimal

Estimate each product.

1. $6.2 \times 9 =$ _____

2. $3 \times 5.3 =$ _____

3. $3.95 \times 7 =$ _____

4. $40 \times 8.6 =$ _____

5. $5.3 \times 2 =$ _____

6. $8 \times 9.9 =$ _____

Round to the greatest place to estimate each product.

7. $32 \times 9.1 =$ _____

8. $16 \times 3.2 =$ _____

9. $8 \times 3.41 =$ _____

10. $11 \times 3.8 =$ _____

11. $19 \times 8.9 =$ _____

12. $8.1 \times 63 =$ _____

Decide if each product will be greater than or less than the estimate. Write $>$ or $<$.

13. 19×3.8

14. 12×8.9

15. 9.1×63

_____

_____

_____

Problem Solving

16. If gasoline costs $1.31 per gallon, about how much will 20 gallons

cost? _____

17. Tiles measure 4.9 cm on each side. About how many tiles will fit on

a line that is 20 cm long? Will the actual number of tiles be less than

or more than this amount? _____

Review and Remember

Tell whether each number is divisible by 2, 3, 4, 5, 6, 9, or 10.

18. 102

19. 365

20. 90,210

21. 3,339

_____

_____

_____

_____

Problem Solving
Multistep Problems

Use the information below to answer each question.
Explain your choices.

Paula had $120 to spend on her garden. She spent $18.95 on vegetable seeds and $34.50 on flowers. She also bought three bags of fertilizer for $39.00 and a new hoe. How much did Paula spend?

1. What information is not needed to find the amount Paula had left after her purchases?

   a. The amount of money Paula started with.

   b. The price of each bag of fertilizer.

   c. The amount she spent on flowers.

2. What must you find to determine the amount Paula had left after her purchases?

   a. The total cost of the items she purchased.

   b. The price of each bag of fertilizer.

   c. The amount of money Paula started with.

3. What information is missing from this problem? _____

4. Which number sentence represents the amount of money that Paula spent?

   a. $120 + $18.95 + $34.50 + $39.00

   b. $18.95 + $34.50 + $39.00

   c. $18.95 + $34.50 + $39.00 + n

Review and Remember

Add or subtract.

5. 0.7
   $+ 3.4$

6. 32.9
   $+ 2.6$

7. 5.03
   $+ 7$

8. 248.97
   $+ 32.56$

9. 4.6
   $- 1.7$

10. 12.3
   $- 7.24$

11. 4.8
   $- 0.555$

12. 6.001
   $- 0.663$

EXPLORE: Investigating Decimal Multiplication

Draw a model to show each multiplication sentence. Then write the product.

1. $0.4 \times 0.3 =$ _____

2. $0.8 \times 0.3 =$ _____

3. $0.2 \times 0.5 =$ _____

4. $0.3 \times 0.7 =$ _____

Problem Solving

5. The odometer on a school bus reads 8934.4 miles at the beginning of a trip. At the end of the trip, it reads 9523.8. How many miles did the school bus travel? _____

6. The school bus holds 52.5 gallons of fuel, which costs $1.44 per gallon. How much does it cost to fill the tank? _____

Review and Remember

Use pencil and paper, mental math, or a calculator to solve.

7. $12 \times 120 =$ _____

8. $14,875 - 693 =$ _____

9. $546 \div 26 =$ _____

10. $81,636 - 29 =$ _____

11. $450 \div 90 =$ _____

12. $526 + 963 =$ _____

Name _____

Multiplying Decimals

Estimate first. Then find the exact product.

1.　5.4
　　× 3.1 _____

2.　3.12
　　× 5.2 _____

3.　0.15
　　× 1.6 _____

4.　2.1
　　× 0.12 _____

5.　8.1
　　× 2.1 _____

6.　0.63
　　× 1.2 _____

7.　7.9
　　× 8.1 _____

8.　5.3
　　× 6.2 _____

Problem Solving

9. Ms. Rodriguez ordered 2.2 pounds of macaroni salad for $2.19 per pound and 1.2 pounds of sliced turkey for $4.99 per pound. How much did the food cost altogether? (Hint: round your answer to the nearest penny.) _____

10. At the museum snack bar, a teacher buys fruit bars for 12 students at a cost of $0.25 per bar. How much change should she get from $5.00? _____

Review and Remember

Find each answer.

11. 28 × 12 = _____

12. $9.02 × 6 = _____

13. 345 × 9 = _____

14. 7.12 × 8 = _____

15. 22 × 27 = _____

16. $12.01 × 3 = _____

Name _____

Multiplication With Zeros in the Product

Multiply.

1. $0.08 \times 0.09 =$ _____

2. $0.05 \times 0.04 =$ _____

3. $0.06 \times 0.03 =$ _____

4. $0.07 \times 0.05 =$ _____

Find each n.

5. $0.08 \times n = 0.0024$ _____

6. $n \times 2.1 = 0.21$ _____

7. $0.21 \times 10 = n$ _____

8. $n \times 0.05 = 0.0025$ _____

Problem Solving

9. The electric company charges $0.09 per kilowatt-hour. If a family used 175.2 kilowatt-hours, what was the cost of the electricity?

_____

10. Some microscopes magnify an object 1,000 times its actual size. If a microorganism is 0.023 mm, what will be its magnified size?

_____

11. Jan mulltiplies 0.06 by 0.02. He says that there are 3 zeros to the right of the decimal point. Is he correct? Explain. _____

_____

Review and Remember

Find each answer.

12. $1.2 - 0.3 =$ _____

13. $8,452 \times 5 =$ _____

14. $\$652 + \$2.98 =$ _____

15. $310 \div 10 =$ _____

16. $4,590 + 3,215 =$ _____

17. $9,909 + 11 =$ _____

Problem Solving
Choose a Strategy

Solve each problem. Try these or other strategies you have learned.
• Draw a Diagram • Find a Pattern • Make a Table • Work Backwards

1. Jason usually pays $4.50 for a car wash. He can buy a book of 6
car-wash coupons for $24.00. How much can he save on car washes

if he buys one book of coupons? _____

2. Kayla's mother gave her $10.00 to spend at the arcade. She spent $4.75
on video games, $1.25 on popcorn, and $0.75 on a lemonade. She let
her friend Sarah borrow $1.50. How much money does Kayla have left?

_____

3. Carlos leaves home for a bicycle ride. He rides 2 blocks east, 3 blocks
south, 6 blocks west, 2 blocks north, and 4 blocks east. Where is he?

_____

4. There are 192 students involved in the Science Fair. They are required
to work on their projects in groups of three or four. What is the smallest
possible number of groups? What is the largest possible number of groups?

_____

5. Mario sold 3 magazine subscriptions on Monday. If sales doubled each
day, how many subscriptions did he sell altogether through Thursday?

_____

Review and Remember

Multiply.

6.	**7.**	**8.**	**9.**
46	24	4,336	654
× 81	× 162	× 9	× 87

Find the average.

10. 9, 7, 23, 9, 17   **11.** 256, 198, 452   **12.** 151, 178, 196

_____   _____   _____

Dividing Decimals by 10, 100, and 1,000

Use patterns to find each quotient.

1. 61.12 ÷ 1 = _____

61.12 ÷ 10 = _____

61.12 ÷ 100 = _____

61.12 ÷ 1,000 = _____

2. 456.3 ÷ 1 = _____

456.3 ÷ 10 = _____

456.3 ÷ 100 = _____

456.3 ÷ 1,000 = _____

3. 52.8 ÷ 1 = _____

52.8 ÷ 10 = _____

52.8 ÷ 100 = _____

52.8 ÷ 1,000 = _____

4. 3.012 ÷ 1 = _____

3.012 ÷ 10 = _____

3.012 ÷ 100 = _____

3.012 ÷ 1,000 = _____

Use patterns to divide.

5. 32.1 ÷ 100 = _____

6. 11.2 ÷ 10 = _____

7. 0.12 ÷ 1000 = _____

Find each *n*.

8. 23.1 ÷ *n* = 2.31

n = _____

9. *n* ÷ 100 = 8.632

n = _____

10. 63.12 ÷ 1 = *n*

n = _____

Problem Solving

11. One hundred collectors cards cost $45.00. How much does each card cost?

_____

12. Animal food at the zoo costs $2.50 for 25 animal pellets. How much does each pellet cost?

_____

Review and Remember

Find each answer.

13. 3.23 + 0.95 + 5.2 = _____

14. $0.98 + $0.63 = _____

15. 56.3 × 1.2 = _____

16. 1.83 + 0.135 + 0.0023 = _____

EXPLORE: Investigating Decimal Division

Use base-ten blocks to find each quotient.

1. $5.62 \div 2 =$ _____   **2.** $3.25 \div 5 =$ _____   **3.** $4.24 \div 4 =$ _____

4. $0.50 \div 2 =$ _____   **5.** $6.36 \div 3 =$ _____   **6.** $7.14 \div 7 =$ _____

7. $8.88 \div 8 =$ _____   **8.** $9.27 \div 9 =$ _____   **9.** $2.10 \div 7 =$ _____

Problem Solving

Use the sign to solve Problems 10–11.

10. How much does one bunch of carrots cost?

_____

11. Which is the better buy, fresh fruit or yogurt with a crunch topping? Explain your reasoning.

_____

_____

_____

_____

ON SALE!	
Carrots	3 bunches for $3.39
Fresh Fruit	**Yogurt with Crunch Topping**
4 Cartons for $3.20	6 Cartons for $3.60

Review and Remember

Compare. Use $>$, $<$, or $=$.

12. $12 \times 2 \bigcirc 3 \times 10$ **13.** $250 \div 5 \bigcirc 200 \div 4$ **14.** $63 \div 9 \bigcirc 72 \div 8$

15. $6 \times 6 \bigcirc 80 \div 2$ **16.** $11 \times 5 \bigcirc 10 \times 6$ **17.** $10 \times 5 \bigcirc 1 \times 50$

Dividing Decimals

Estimate. Then find the exact quotient.

1. $2.32 ÷ 2 = _____ **2.** 1.56 ÷ 12 = _____ **3.** 32.2 ÷ 14 = _____

Divide.

4. 7)35.7 **5.** 25)30.75 **6.** 41)875.76

7. 19)100.7 **8.** 11)12.122 **9.** 16)25.6

10. 48.3 ÷ 23 = _____ **11.** 138.15 ÷ 15 = _____ **12.** 218.66 ÷ 26 = _____

Problem Solving

13. A carton of paper costs $73.20. There are 12 packages of paper in each carton. How much does each package cost? _____

14. One brand of floppy disks costs $21.10 for a box of 10 disks. Another brand costs $14.94 for a box of 6 disks. Which is the better buy? Explain your reasoning.

_____

_____

_____

Review and Remember

Identify each plane figure.

15.

16.
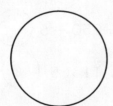

17.
_____

_____ _____ _____

Problem Solving
Choose a Computation Method

Use the information from the table below. Decide whether you will use estimation, mental math, paper and pencil, or a calculator to solve Problems 1–6.

1. Emily bought a poster and a key chain for each of her twin sisters. How much did she spend?

_____

2. Mark has $5.00 from his allowance to spend. What is the greatest number of different items Mark can buy?

_____

3. Mark decides that he will buy two different items with his $5.00. What combinations of items can he buy?

_____

Gift Shop Prices	
Item	**Price**
T-shirts	$7.95
Hats	$9.75
Key chains	$2.25
Pens	$1.35
Calendars	$1.50
Postcards	$0.65
Posters	$1.99

4. Lorena has $19.10 to spend. If she buys a hat and a T-shirt, does she have enough money left to buy anything else?

_____

5. Last week, the shop sold 18 hats. If they make $3.50 profit on each hat, how much profit did they make on hat sales?

_____

6. If the school decides to purchase a hat, a T-shirt, and a poster for each student, about how much will they spend per student?

_____

Review and Remember

Use the drawing at the right to name an example of each geometric figure.

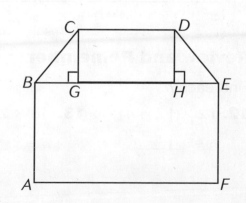

7. a triangle _____

8. a quadrilateral _____

9. a hexagon _____

10. right angle _____

EXPLORE: Primes and Composites

Write whether each number is prime or composite.

Give an example to show why the number is composite.

1. 27 _____   **2.** 31 _____   **3.** 35 _____

4. 51 _____   **5.** 59 _____   **6.** 80 _____

7. 73 _____   **8.** 49 _____   **9.** 61 _____

Problem Solving

10. Sieve of Eratosthenes

Use a hundred chart. Cross out 1. Circle the next number. Then cross out all of the multiples of that number. Circle the next number that is not crossed out and cross out all of the multiples of that number. Continue until all of the numbers are either circled or crossed out. In your own words, explain the difference between the circled numbers and those that are crossed out.

_____

_____

_____

11. Mrs. Ray has 12 hours to schedule 7 auditions. If each audition takes about 2 hours, does she have enough time to complete them? Explain your answer.

_____

Review and Remember

Find each *n*.

12. $12 \times 12 = n$ **13.** $48 \times 2 = n$ **14.** $n = 3 \times 19$ **15.** $n = 25 \times 4$

n = _____   *n* = _____   *n* = _____   *n* = _____

Common Factors and Greatest Common Factors

List the factors of each number. Find the common factors of each set of numbers.

1. 10 and 12

2. 24 and 30

3. 12 and 32

_____   _____   _____

_____   _____   _____

_____   _____   _____

_____   _____   _____

_____   _____   _____

Find the GCF of each set of numbers.

4. 12 and 48

5. 35 and 42

6. 15 and 24

7. 16 and 20

_____   _____   _____   _____

Problem Solving

8. Draw a Venn diagram that shows the GCF of 30, 40, and 48.

9. Janet has 56 red tulip bulbs. Janele has 40 yellow tulip bulbs. Each girl wants to plant a rectangular garden with the same number of bulbs in each row in both gardens. How many bulbs will be in a row of each garden? Use a drawing to explain your answer.

_____

_____

Review and Remember

Use mental math to find the answer.

10. $45 \div 5 =$ _____

11. $32 \div 4 =$ _____

12. $72 \div 8 =$ _____

13. $420 \div 6 =$ _____

14. $1,000 \div 5 =$ _____

15. $210 \div 7 =$ _____

Common Multiples and Least Common Multiples

Find the LCM of each set of numbers.

1. 4 and 8

2. 4 and 9

3. 6 and 5

4. 10 and 15

_____

_____

_____

_____

5. 12 and 18

6. 5 and 30

7. 3, 4, and 6

8. 6, 8, and 12

_____

_____

_____

_____

Problem Solving

9. The play *Fiddler on the Roof* is at a local theater for two weeks. Roberta would like to see the play with her sister. Roberta has every fourth day off from work. Her sister has every sixth day off. Will they get to see the play together? Explain your answer using LCM.

_____

_____

_____

10. Henry has every third day off. He wants to see the play together with Roberta and her sister. Is this possible? Explain your answer using LCM.

_____

_____

_____

11. There are two shows of *Fiddler on the Roof* each day. If Mark performs one and one half hours during each show, how many hours will he perform in two weeks?

_____

Review and Remember

Solve for *n*.

12. $400 \times 60 = n$

13. $1,388 \times 4 = n$

14. $n \times n = 64$

$n = $ _____

$n = $ _____

$n = $ _____

Problem Solving
Reasonable Answers

Read the paragraph and answer each question.

The school band is preparing for its annual spring concert. They are going to sell T-shirts after the performance. The band members agreed to order 200 shirts and have $\frac{1}{2}$ of the shirts red, $\frac{1}{4}$ of the shirts blue, and $\frac{1}{4}$ of the shirts green.

1. Is it reasonable to say that the band will sell 60 blue T-shirts?

Explain why or why not. _____

2. Is it reasonable to say that the band will sell 100 red T-shirts?

Explain why or why not. _____

3. If the T-shirts sell for $8 each, could the band members make $500 from selling

green T-shirts? _____

4. After the concert was over, there were only 10 T-shirts left. The cost of the T-shirts to the band was $1,200. Did the band make money, break even, or lose money?

_____

Review and Remember

Use mental math to solve.

5. $40 \times 20 =$ _____

6. $180 \div 90 =$ _____

7. $\$10 - \$3.50 =$ _____

8. $750 \div 25 =$ _____

9. $45 \times 20 =$ _____

10. $52 + 48 =$ _____

Relating Fractions and Decimals

Write a fraction and decimal for each shaded part.

1.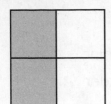

2.

3.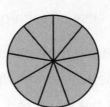

4.

_____   _____   _____   _____

	Word Form	Fraction Notation	Decimal Notation
5.	two tenths		0.2
6.			4.1
7.	two and seven tenths		2.7
8.		$3\frac{9}{10}$	

Problem Solving

9. Mr. Fuller's class is reading *Hatchet*. There are 25 students in his class. Of those students, 15 have finished the book. What fraction of the class has not finished the book?

_____

10. Marcus and his 4 brothers each eat one of eight slices of pizza. Is more or less than half of the pizza left for their parents?

_____

Review and Remember

Compare. Write >, <, or =.

11. 13.45 ◯ 13.045   **12.** 168 ◯ 1,680   **13.** 14 × 2 ◯ 13 × 2

14. 1.08 ◯ 1.080   **15.** 101.1 ◯ 11.01   **16.** 13.05 ◯ 13.005

EXPLORE: Relating Fractions to One Half and One

Compare. Write $<$, $>$, or $=$ for each.

1. $\frac{3}{4}$ ◯ $\frac{1}{2}$

2. $\frac{3}{9}$ ◯ $\frac{1}{2}$

3. $\frac{8}{16}$ ◯ $\frac{1}{2}$

4. $\frac{1}{2}$ ◯ $\frac{1}{3}$

5. $\frac{1}{2}$ ◯ $\frac{3}{7}$

6. $\frac{6}{12}$ ◯ $\frac{1}{2}$

7. $\frac{1}{2}$ ◯ $\frac{10}{20}$

8. $\frac{5}{11}$ ◯ $\frac{1}{2}$

Problem Solving

Use the chart at the right to answer Problems 9–11.

9. During the week, it rained five days in a row. On what day did it rain the most?

_____

10. On what day did it rain the least?

_____

Rainfall	
Day	Inches of Rain
Monday	3/6
Tuesday	1/3
Wednesday	7/8
Thursday	3/7
Friday	4/8

11. On what days did it rain the same amount? _____

Review and Remember

Round each number to the underlined place.

12. 69.1<u>8</u>

13. 1<u>5</u>.62

14. 19<u>9</u>.57

15. 10<u>8</u>.09

16. <u>1</u>,468,342

17. 26.0<u>0</u>8

18. 307.<u>0</u>8

19. 455.5<u>6</u>8

Solve for n.

20. $n = 8 \times 2 + 8 \times 4 - 36$

$n = $ _____

21. $n = 8 - 5 + 3 - 6$

$n = $ _____

RETA E. KING LIBRARY

Fractions Greater Than One

Write each mixed number as an improper fraction.

1. $1\frac{5}{8}$ **2.** $4\frac{2}{5}$ **3.** $2\frac{1}{7}$ **4.** $5\frac{5}{6}$ **5.** $8\frac{1}{7}$

_____   _____   _____   _____   _____

Write each improper fraction as a mixed number.

6. $\frac{25}{3}$ **7.** $\frac{51}{10}$ **8.** $\frac{32}{7}$ **9.** $\frac{22}{3}$ **10.** $\frac{55}{8}$

_____   _____   _____   _____   _____

Problem Solving

11. Mr. Morillo is buying popcorn for 28 fifth graders in the theater. He can carry 5 boxes of popcorn at one time. Write an improper fraction that shows how many trips Mr. Morillo must make to the concession stand.

_____

12. In Problem 11, how many trips does Mr. Morillo actually have to make to the concession stand? Explain your answer.

_____

13. The fifth graders fill up $3\frac{1}{2}$ rows in the theater. How many students are in each full row? (Hint: write the mixed number as an improper fraction.)

_____

Review and Remember

Find the quotient.

14. $22\overline{)756}$ **15.** $34\overline{)8,934}$ **16.** $100\overline{)6,000}$

17. $14\overline{)3,642}$ **18.** $13\overline{)3,582}$ **19.** $45\overline{)65,200}$

Problem Solving
Make a List

Make a list to answer Problems 1–4.

1. Jack, Maria, José, and Beth were introduced and shook hands.

   How many different handshakes occurred? _____

2. Beth is painting a portrait of Jack, Maria, and José. Each of the

   three could either be sitting or standing. How many different

   paintings could be done with the different combinations? _____

3. At a restaurant, Lee ordered a hamburger and french fries. The

   three toppings that he ordered were bacon, lettuce, and tomato.

   How many different ways could these toppings be stacked? _____

4. A blue car and a red car are parked beside each other.
   The cars can either be facing east or west.

   How many different east-west combinations can the cars be parked? _____

Review and Remember
Find the answer.

5. 18 + 24 = ____   **6.** 13 − 9 = ____   **7.** 36 ÷ 4 = ____   **8.** 8 × 9 = ____

9. 51 ÷ 17 = ____   **10.** 5 × 14 = ____   **11.** 88 − 11 = ____   **12.** 62 + 13 = ____

Equivalent Fractions

Replace each △ with a number that will make the fractions equivalent.

1. $\frac{2}{3} = \frac{\triangle}{18}$ **2.** $\frac{16}{24} = \frac{2}{\triangle}$ **3.** $\frac{6}{7} = \frac{\triangle}{42}$ **4.** $\frac{3}{6} = \frac{\triangle}{2}$

_____   _____   _____   _____

5. $\frac{3}{5} = \frac{\triangle}{15}$ **6.** $\frac{4}{9} = \frac{32}{\triangle}$ **7.** $\frac{18}{27} = \frac{2}{\triangle}$ **8.** $\frac{9}{27} = \frac{1}{\triangle}$

_____   _____   _____   _____

Problem Solving

9. A billboard is made up of 24 sections. Each section costs $300. If an advertiser made a $5,000 deposit to construct the billboard, how much money is owed when the job is complete?

_____

10. The construction company can complete 4 sections of the billboard in a day. After 5 days, what fraction of the billboard has been completed?

_____

Review and Remember

Estimate each answer.

11.   2,689
   + 3,462 _____

12.   15,839
   62,329
   + 10,000 _____

13.   5,683
   − 3,210 _____

14.   14.89
   16.35
   + 12.93 _____

15.   24,358
   + 98,342 _____

16.   839
   − 578 _____

17.   6,034
   4,058
   + 5,932 _____

18.   7,832
   ×   32 _____

19.   4,921
   ×   18 _____

Fractions in Simplest Form

Write each fraction in simplest form. Write *yes* if the fraction is already in simplest form.

1. $\frac{15}{25}$

2. $\frac{4}{16}$

3. $\frac{6}{11}$

_____

_____

_____

4. $\frac{48}{56}$

5. $\frac{9}{22}$

6. $\frac{12}{18}$

_____

_____

_____

7. $\frac{3}{9}$

8. $\frac{14}{16}$

9. $\frac{12}{15}$

_____

_____

_____

Problem Solving

10. Cathy sold 100 tickets to a play. If 60 tickets were adult tickets, what fraction of the

tickets sold were children's tickets? Write your answer in simplest form. _____

11. In Problem 10, if adult tickets cost $3.50 and student tickets cost $1.50, how

much money did Cathy collect? _____

Review and Remember

Find the GCF of each set of numbers.

12. 12 and 16

13. 18 and 20

14. 25 and 30

_____

_____

_____

15. 14 and 21

16. 18 and 36

17. 6 and 15

_____

_____

_____

18. 8 and 12

19. 35 and 70

20. 24 and 42

_____

_____

_____

Comparing and Ordering Fractions and Mixed Numbers

Compare. Write $>$, $<$, or $=$ for each.

1. $\frac{3}{6}$ ◯ $\frac{5}{10}$ **2.** $\frac{2}{3}$ ◯ $\frac{3}{8}$ **3.** $\frac{4}{5}$ ◯ $\frac{6}{7}$ **4.** $\frac{10}{12}$ ◯ $\frac{5}{6}$

Order the fractions from least to greatest.

5. $\frac{3}{8}$, $\frac{1}{4}$, and $\frac{1}{2}$ **6.** $\frac{3}{10}$, $\frac{1}{2}$, and $\frac{4}{5}$ **7.** $\frac{1}{3}$, $\frac{4}{5}$, and $\frac{5}{6}$

_____ _____ _____

8. $\frac{1}{6}$, $\frac{1}{3}$, and $\frac{1}{8}$ **9.** $\frac{3}{6}$, $\frac{3}{5}$, and $\frac{3}{7}$ **10.** $\frac{8}{9}$, $\frac{6}{7}$, and $\frac{4}{5}$

_____ _____ _____

Problem Solving

11. Omar had $5\frac{2}{5}$ pages of lines to learn for the class play. Jeremy had $5\frac{1}{3}$ pages, and Celia had $5\frac{3}{8}$ pages. Which student had the greatest number of lines to learn?

_____

12. During intermission at the class play, Jared bought three hot dogs for $1.50 each. He also bought a soda for $0.75 and a bag of chips for $0.50. How much change should he get back from $10.00? _____

Review and Remember

Write each fraction in lowest terms.

13. $\frac{14}{35}$ **14.** $\frac{15}{18}$ **15.** $\frac{24}{36}$ **16.** $\frac{20}{30}$

_____ _____ _____ _____

17. $\frac{21}{27}$ **18.** $\frac{56}{64}$ **19.** $\frac{49}{70}$ **20.** $\frac{16}{24}$

_____ _____ _____ _____

Problem Solving
Finding Fraction Patterns

Answer each question.

1. When Shannon was 10, her parents decided to give her an amount of money equal to $\frac{1}{2}$ of her age for her allowance. Then the next year she received $\frac{1}{3}$ of her age, the next year $\frac{1}{4}$ of her age, and so on. If the pattern continues, how old will Shannon be when she receives $\frac{1}{9}$ of her age? _____

2. The width of the bottom level of a pyramid is $\frac{1}{3}$ the length. The next level is $\frac{1}{6}$ the length, and the next is $\frac{1}{12}$ the length. By what fraction of the length is the width of the 6th level? _____

3. The tree in Erin's front yard is decorated with one long strand of lights. The bottom of the tree has $\frac{1}{3}$ of the strand of lights, the next level of branches has $\frac{1}{5}$ of the strand of lights, and the next has $\frac{1}{7}$. How many levels are there if the top of the tree has $\frac{1}{11}$ of the strand of lights? _____

4. Books are stacked on top of each other. The top book is 10 cm in length, the book below it is 20 cm in length, and the book below that is 40 cm in length. How many books are there in the stack if the bottom book is 80 cm in length? _____

Review and Remember

Find the answer.

5. $23 + 38 =$ _____

6. $6 \times 4 =$ _____

7. $35 - 15 =$ _____

8. $56 \div 7 =$ _____

9. $24 - 12 =$ _____

10. $4 \times 9 =$ _____

11. $42 \div 6 =$ _____

12. $19 + 41 =$ _____

13. $8 \times 8 =$ _____

Adding Fractions and Mixed Numbers: Like Denominators

Add. Write each answer in simplest form.

1. $\dfrac{3}{11}$
$+ \dfrac{4}{11}$

2. $\dfrac{3}{8}$
$+ \dfrac{3}{8}$

3. $\dfrac{2}{9}$
$+ \dfrac{7}{9}$

4. $\dfrac{5}{6}$
$+ \dfrac{5}{6}$

5. $1\dfrac{3}{5}$
$+ 2\dfrac{1}{5}$

6. $3\dfrac{1}{7}$
$+ 4\dfrac{6}{7}$

7. $4\dfrac{3}{4}$
$+ 2\dfrac{3}{4}$

8. $4\dfrac{2}{9}$
$+ 6\dfrac{4}{9}$

Problem Solving

9. Cassandra is baking two cakes for the bake sale. One cake mix calls for $2\dfrac{3}{4}$ cups of flour. The other mix calls for $2\dfrac{1}{4}$ cups of flour. How many cups of flour does she need in all? _____

10. Cassandra can sell her cakes whole for $3.00 each. If she cuts each cake into eight slices, she can sell each slice for $0.50. How much more money can she make by selling slices rather than whole cakes? _____

Review and Remember

Add.

11. $\begin{array}{r} 15{,}237 \\ 6{,}823 \\ + \ 4{,}050 \\ \hline \end{array}$

12. $\begin{array}{r} 15.689 \\ + \ 2.38 \\ \hline \end{array}$

13. $\begin{array}{r} 4{,}634 \\ 276 \\ + 1{,}200 \\ \hline \end{array}$

14. $\begin{array}{r} 134.891 \\ + \ 2.009 \\ \hline \end{array}$

15. $14.08 + 0.134 =$ _____

16. $6.83 + 0.48 + 6 =$ _____

Subtracting Fractions and Mixed Numbers: Like Denominators

Subtract. Write each answer in simplest form.

1. $\dfrac{8}{15}$
$-\dfrac{3}{15}$

2. $1\dfrac{3}{4}$
$-\dfrac{1}{4}$

3. $4\dfrac{5}{9}$
$-2\dfrac{3}{9}$

4. $7\dfrac{3}{8}$
$-4\dfrac{3}{8}$

5. $6\dfrac{4}{7}$
$-2\dfrac{6}{7}$

6. $8\dfrac{1}{4}$
$-6\dfrac{3}{4}$

7. 8
$-7\dfrac{2}{3}$

8. $6\dfrac{5}{12}$
$-4\dfrac{7}{12}$

Problem Solving

9. Mariah lives $2\dfrac{7}{10}$ miles from school. Her friend Rhonda lives $3\dfrac{3}{10}$ miles from school. How much farther away from school does Rhonda live? _____

10. The library is $1\dfrac{1}{10}$ miles east of Fox School. Tom lives $2\dfrac{3}{10}$ miles west of Fox School. Tom plans to walk to the library after school and then walk home. How far will he walk in all after school? Make a drawing to explain your answer.

_____

Review and Remember

Subtract.

11. $7{,}342$
$-\quad141$

12. $8{,}600$
$-\quad246$

13. 403
-196

14. $60{,}003$
$-14{,}581$

15. $143.8 - 24.6 =$ _____

16. $18 - 1.34 =$ _____

Problem Solving
Too Much or Too Little Information

Answer each question for which you have enough information. If you have too little information, tell what information is missing.

Owen and Juan are planning to drive to a horse ranch to feed the horses.
They leave at 11:00 a.m. and drive 48 miles per hour. The ranch is 36 miles away.
For the horses they packed $\frac{3}{4}$ pound of hay, $\frac{1}{3}$ pound of carrots, and $\frac{1}{4}$ pound of apples.
The total cost of the hay, carrots, and apples was $10.50.

1. What time do Owen and Juan arrive at the ranch? _____

2. How much did the hay and carrots cost? _____

_____

3. The horses ate $\frac{1}{2}$ pound of hay and $\frac{1}{8}$ pound of apples. How much food do

Owen and Juan go home with? _____

_____

4. What time do Owen and Juan arrive back at home? _____

_____

Review and Remember

Use mental math to solve.

5. $3.50 + $2.50 = _____   **6.** 25 × 2 = _____   **7.** 70 ÷ 2 = _____

8. 26 − 16 = _____   **9.** 620 ÷ 31 = _____   **10.** 96 + 54 = _____

Estimating Sums and Differences of Mixed Numbers

Estimate each sum or difference.

1. $3\frac{3}{4}$
$+ 2\frac{1}{4}$

2. $8\frac{2}{5}$
$+ 6\frac{4}{5}$

3. $6\frac{1}{3}$
$- 2\frac{1}{3}$

4. $10\frac{8}{16}$
$- 6\frac{4}{16}$

5. 5
$- 3\frac{7}{12}$

6. $8\frac{4}{5}$
$+ 7\frac{3}{5}$

7. 8
$+ 9\frac{7}{10}$

8. $4\frac{1}{6}$
$- 3\frac{5}{6}$

Problem Solving

Decide if you can use an estimate or need an exact answer to solve each problem. Then solve.

9. Alyssa is making fruit salad. She has $2\frac{3}{4}$ lb of grapes, $1\frac{1}{4}$ lb of apples, $2\frac{1}{4}$ lb of cantaloupe, and $3\frac{3}{4}$ lb of watermelon. How many pounds of fruit salad will she make? _____

10. If it costs $2.89 per lb to make fruit salad, how much did Alyssa spend on the salad in Problem 9? _____

Review and Remember

Multiply.

11. 239
$\times 201$

12. $4,006$
$\times\ \ 20$

13. $1,903$
$\times\ \ 19$

14. $24,000$
$\times\ \ 300$

15. 16.3
$\times 0.4$

16. 2.8
$\times 1.2$

17. 23
$\times 0.84$

18. 2.001
$\times 4.32$

EXPLORE: Working With Fractions With Unlike Denominators

Use fraction pieces or draw diagrams to find each sum or difference.

1. $\frac{1}{6} + \frac{2}{3} =$ _____

2. $\frac{4}{5} + \frac{1}{10} =$ _____

3. $\frac{3}{4} + \frac{1}{6} =$ _____

4. $\frac{3}{4} + \frac{1}{12} =$ _____

5. $\frac{2}{4} - \frac{1}{2} =$ _____

6. $\frac{3}{8} - \frac{1}{4} =$ _____

7. $\frac{2}{3} - \frac{4}{9} =$ _____

8. $\frac{3}{4} - \frac{2}{3} =$ _____

9. $\frac{1}{8} + \frac{2}{3} =$ _____

Problem Solving

Use the drawing at the right to answer Problems 10–12.

10. What part of the pizza has pepperoni

or sausage? _____

11. Joshua only likes pepperoni pizza. What fractional part of the whole

pizza does he not like? _____

12. What part of the pizza has no meat on it? _____

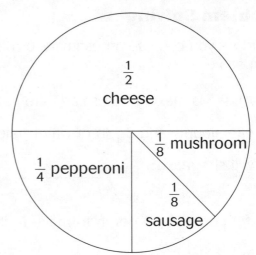

Review and Remember

Divide.

13. $60\overline{)4,800}$

14. $2\overline{)2,438}$

15. $21\overline{)1,483}$

16. $21\overline{)2,304}$

17. $2\overline{)16.2}$

18. $0.5\overline{)25.85}$

19. $0.3\overline{)258}$

20. $1.5\overline{)39.195}$

Name _____

Adding Fractions With Unlike Denominators

Add. Simplify each sum if possible.

1. $\frac{2}{3}$
$+\frac{3}{4}$

2. $\frac{7}{8}$
$+\frac{5}{6}$

3. $\frac{3}{5}$
$+\frac{1}{4}$

4. $\frac{3}{10}$
$+\frac{3}{4}$

5. $\frac{3}{4}$
$+\frac{1}{6}$

6. $\frac{3}{7}$
$+\frac{2}{14}$

7. $\frac{4}{5}$
$+\frac{2}{3}$

8. $\frac{5}{6}$
$+\frac{7}{9}$

Problem Solving

9. Jamie spent $\frac{3}{4}$ hour on her math homework, $\frac{1}{2}$ hour on her science homework, and $\frac{1}{3}$ hour on her social studies homework. How much time did she spend doing homework? _____

10. Jalen spends 2 hours each night on homework. Last night he spent $1\frac{1}{6}$ hours working on his science project. How much time did he spend on other subjects?

_____

Review and Remember

Find the GCF.

11. 16 and 24

12. 20 and 30

13. 18 and 27

14. 24 and 48

_____   _____   _____   _____

Find the LCM.

15. 6 and 9

16. 10 and 15

17. 2, 4, and 6

18. 8 and 9

_____   _____   _____   _____

Subtracting Fractions With Unlike Denominators

Subtract. Simplify when possible.

1. $\frac{5}{6}$
    $-\frac{1}{3}$

2. $\frac{3}{7}$
    $-\frac{1}{14}$

3. $\frac{7}{9}$
    $-\frac{4}{6}$

4. $\frac{2}{10}$
    $-\frac{1}{5}$

5. $\frac{2}{3}$
    $-\frac{3}{5}$

6. $\frac{3}{4}$
    $-\frac{1}{3}$

7. $\frac{4}{5}$
    $-\frac{1}{2}$

8. $\frac{5}{8}$
    $-\frac{2}{6}$

Problem Solving

9. Marisol needs $\frac{3}{4}$ yd of material to make her bookmark. She has $\frac{3}{5}$ yd of her favorite material. How much more material does she need? _____

10. Marisol buys $\frac{1}{2}$ yd of material. How much extra material does she have? _____

11. Danielle bought 2 yd of material at $2.98 per yard, 6 buttons for $0.29 each, and a spool of thread for $1.29. How much change will she receive if she gives the cashier 2 five-dollar bills? _____

Review and Remember

Compare. Use <, >, or =.

12. $\frac{2}{3}$ ◯ $\frac{4}{6}$

13. $\frac{5}{8}$ ◯ $\frac{3}{4}$

14. $\frac{5}{7}$ ◯ $\frac{3}{4}$

15. $1\frac{2}{3}$ ◯ $2\frac{1}{3}$

16. $\frac{4}{5}$ ◯ $\frac{3}{10}$

17. $\frac{5}{10}$ ◯ $\frac{1}{2}$

18. $2\frac{3}{5}$ ◯ $3\frac{3}{5}$

19. $2\frac{4}{8}$ ◯ $2\frac{5}{10}$

20. $8\frac{1}{9}$ ◯ $7\frac{3}{8}$

Adding Mixed Numbers

Add. Simplify each sum, if possible.

1. $5\frac{2}{12}$
    $+ 3\frac{1}{6}$

2. $3\frac{2}{5}$
    $+ 4\frac{1}{3}$

3. $6\frac{2}{3}$
    $+ 4\frac{4}{6}$

4. $10\frac{8}{9}$
    $+ 3\frac{4}{6}$

5. $2\frac{2}{3}$
    $+ 3\frac{4}{7}$

6. $3\frac{3}{4}$
    $+ 2\frac{3}{5}$

7. $\frac{2}{4}$
    $+ 5\frac{1}{3}$

8. $9\frac{5}{8}$
    $+ 3\frac{2}{3}$

Problem Solving

9. Peter wants to ship at least 10 pounds of mixed nuts as a holiday gift. He buys $4\frac{3}{4}$ lb of cashews, $2\frac{1}{2}$ lb of peanuts, and $3\frac{2}{3}$ lb of walnuts. Did he buy enough nuts? _____

10. Suppose it costs $3.00 per lb to ship a package. About how much will it cost Peter to ship the nuts he bought in Problem 9? _____

Review and Remember

Round each number to the underlined place.

11. 1.6<u>8</u>2

12. 13<u>0</u>.486

13. 4<u>6</u>.58

14. 168.<u>3</u>2

15. 10<u>4</u>.89

16. 19.9<u>9</u>5

17. <u>2</u>0.134

18. 163.<u>2</u>59

Subtracting Mixed Numbers

Subtract. Simplify, if possible.

1. $4\frac{6}{10}$
   $- 2\frac{1}{5}$

2. $6\frac{1}{2}$
   $- 2\frac{1}{4}$

3. $5\frac{3}{7}$
   $- 2\frac{2}{3}$

4. $12\frac{1}{5}$
   $- 2\frac{2}{3}$

5. 8
   $- 2\frac{3}{4}$

6. $9\frac{2}{3}$
   $- 7$

7. $8\frac{2}{8}$
   $- 2\frac{2}{4}$

8. $6\frac{2}{3}$
   $- 3\frac{3}{4}$

Problem Solving

9. It takes about $5\frac{2}{5}$ hours to rake the whole yard. If Ming Lee's brother rakes for $2\frac{1}{2}$ hours, how many hours will she have to rake to finish the job?

_____

10. Michael read $\frac{1}{3}$ of his book on Monday, $\frac{1}{6}$ on Tuesday, and $\frac{1}{4}$ on Wednesday. How much of the book does he have left to read?

_____

Review and Remember

Write a decimal for each fraction.

11. $\frac{2}{5}$ _____

12. $\frac{5}{8}$ _____

13. $\frac{3}{4}$ _____

14. $\frac{1}{5}$ _____

15. $\frac{8}{25}$ _____

16. $\frac{5}{20}$ _____

17. $\frac{3}{10}$ _____

18. $\frac{4}{1000}$ _____

Problem Solving
Solve a Simpler Problem

Answer each question.

1. There are 10 rows of houses in a development. In the first row there are 3 houses. In the second row there are 5 houses. In the third row there are 7 houses, and so on. How many houses are in the development? _____

2. Kevin bought 7 different types of dried fruit. He wants to pick 2 of these to put in his trail mix. In how many ways can he choose 2 different dried fruit varieties from the 7 he bought? _____

3. Boxes of produce are labeled on the top and right side of each box. How many labels can you see if there are 8 rows of boxes stacked 3 deep? _____

4. In a swimming pool with 8 lanes, the first lane has 2 swimmers, the second lane has 4 swimmers and the third lane has 6 swimmers. If the pattern continues, how many swimmers are there in the pool? _____

Review and Remember

Round to the nearest tenth.

5. 11.93 _____   6. 9.87 _____   7. 4.67 _____   8. 2.12 _____

9. 5.09 _____   10. 8.26 _____   11. 3.44 _____   12. 5.55 _____

13. 3.43 _____   14. 6.28 _____   15. 12.79 _____   16. 7.23 _____

Multiplying Whole Numbers and Fractions

Multiply. Simplify each product, if possible.

1. $\frac{1}{2} \times 40 =$ _____

2. $\frac{2}{3} \times 27 =$ _____

3. $56 \times \frac{1}{7} =$ _____

4. $\frac{7}{10} \times 100 =$ _____

5. $16 \times \frac{3}{4} =$ _____

6. $\frac{2}{5} \times 12 =$ _____

7. $\frac{3}{8} \times 7 =$ _____

8. $6 \times \frac{3}{5} =$ _____

9. $8 \times \frac{3}{16} =$ _____

10. $12 \times \frac{4}{5} =$ _____

11. $9 \times \frac{3}{11} =$ _____

12. $18 \times \frac{1}{2} =$ _____

Problem Solving

13. There are 258 students at Wood School. About $\frac{2}{3}$ of the students like pizza.

How many students like pizza? _____

14. Of the students in Problem 13 who like pizza, only $\frac{1}{4}$ like mushroom pizza.

How many students like mushroom pizza? _____

15. Of the students in Problem 13 who don't like pizza, $\frac{1}{2}$ are girls. How many girls don't

like pizza? _____

Review and Remember

Solve.

16. $16 - 8 \times 2 + 3 =$ _____

17. $14 \div 7 + 2 \times 3 =$ _____

18. $4 + 6 \div 3 - 3 =$ _____

19. $2 \times (3 + 5) =$ _____

20. $16 + 2 \times 3 - 4 \times 1 =$ _____

21. $15 - 4 + 2 \times 3 =$ _____

EXPLORE: Modeling Fraction Multiplication

Find each product. Make a diagram or use your rule.

1. $\frac{1}{3} \times \frac{1}{4} =$ _____

2. $\frac{2}{3} \times \frac{3}{4} =$ _____

3. $\frac{1}{2} \times \frac{5}{8} =$ _____

4. $\frac{2}{5} \times \frac{5}{7} =$ _____

5. $\frac{5}{6} \times \frac{3}{8} =$ _____

6. $\frac{1}{2} \times \frac{1}{4} =$ _____

7. $\frac{2}{9} \times \frac{3}{4} =$ _____

8. $\frac{1}{5} \times \frac{1}{4} =$ _____

9. $\frac{2}{5} \times \frac{3}{4} =$ _____

10. $\frac{8}{15} \times \frac{1}{3} =$ _____

11. $\frac{1}{10} \times \frac{4}{5} =$ _____

12. $\frac{6}{7} \times \frac{1}{11} =$ _____

Problem Solving

13. The parents of Mrs. Foster's class donated 12 cakes for the bake sale. In the morning, $\frac{1}{3}$ of the cakes were sold. In the afternoon, $\frac{3}{4}$ of the remaining cakes were sold. How many cakes were left over? _____

14. Mrs. Foster's favorite cake recipe calls for 2 cups of flour. She only has $\frac{2}{3}$ of the flour that she needs. How many cups of flour does she have to borrow from her neighbor? _____

Review and Remember

Solve for n.

15. $(16 + n) + 32 = 16 + (4 + 32)$

$n =$ _____

16. $n \times (4 + 3) = (2 \times 4) + (2 \times 3)$

$n =$ _____

17. $n + 18 = 18$

$n =$ _____

18. $n \times 643 = 643$

$n =$ _____

19. $16 \times n = 0$

$n =$ _____

20. $n \times 20 = 60$

$n =$ _____

Multiplying Fractions and Mixed Numbers

Multiply. Simplify each product, if possible.

1. $\frac{2}{5} \times 1\frac{2}{3} =$ _____

2. $3 \times 5\frac{1}{2} =$ _____

3. $\frac{3}{4} \times 6\frac{1}{2} =$ _____

4. $2\frac{2}{5} \times 1\frac{1}{4} =$ _____

5. $3\frac{3}{7} \times 2\frac{2}{6} =$ _____

6. $9\frac{1}{2} \times 7 =$ _____

7. $6\frac{2}{8} \times 5\frac{1}{5} =$ _____

8. $2\frac{1}{2} \times \frac{5}{6} =$ _____

9. $5\frac{3}{4} \times 8 =$ _____

Problem Solving

10. Erin's mom went to the orchard to pick some apples. She brought home $4\frac{2}{3}$ lb of apples. She used $\frac{3}{4}$ of the apples to bake a pie. How many pounds of apples were left over?

_____

11. The apples in Problem 10 cost $0.60 per lb. How much did Erin's mom pay for the apples?

_____

Review and Remember

Find the average of each set of numbers.

12. 25, 15, 18, 34, 41

_____

13. 26.7, 36.1, 29.3

_____

14. 550, 830, 630, 640

_____

15. 1.26, 3.6, 8.12, 6.9

_____

16. 8, 4, 13, 4, 4, 3

_____

17. 0.63, 0.86, 0.88

_____

EXPLORE: Dividing by Fractions

Use fraction pieces or a diagram to find each answer.

1. $\frac{3}{4} \div \frac{1}{12} =$ _____

2. $\frac{2}{3} \div \frac{1}{6} =$ _____

3. $3 \div \frac{1}{5} =$ _____

4. $1 \div \frac{1}{8} =$ _____

5. $\frac{1}{2} \div \frac{1}{4} =$ _____

6. $3 \div \frac{1}{4} =$ _____

Problem Solving

Use the recipe at the right to answer Problems 7–8.

7. If Mario wants to make one dozen muffins, how much flour does he need?

_____

8. If Mario wants to make 3 dozen muffins, how much milk does he need?

_____

Apple Muffins	
$1\frac{1}{2}$ c milk	2 tbsp baking soda
2 eggs	2 tbsp cinnamon
$\frac{1}{2}$ c shortening	$\frac{2}{3}$ c raisins
$4\frac{1}{2}$ c flour	2 c chopped apple
Bake 350°	45 min
Makes two dozen muffins	

Review and Remember

Rule: Multiply by 0.4

9.	0.23	
10.	4.2	
11.		1.216
12.		2.8

Rule: Divide by 1.2

13.	4.08	
14.		120
15.	0.036	
16.	6	

Problem Solving
Representing Remainders

For each problem express the remainder as a fraction, a decimal, or a whole number. Tell why you chose the method you did. Then solve the problem.

1. Mr. Kelly bought 50 doughnuts to bring to school for the students. The total cost of

the doughnuts was $15.95. What is the cost of one doughnut? _____

_____

2. Ms. Jackson and her class of 25 students are going on a camping trip. Ms. Jackson

is going to pack 3-person tents. How many tents does she have to pack? _____

_____

3. The campgrounds that Ms. Jackson and her class are going to are 137.5 miles away.

How long will it take the class to get there if the bus travels at 55 mph? _____

_____

4. Theresa and Kyle put together 370 model airplanes. They used 560 tubes of glue.

How many tubes of glue did they use on each plane? _____

_____

Review and Remember

Use mental math to solve.

5. $100 \div 25 =$ _____

6. $75 \times 2 =$ _____

7. $50 - $25 =$ _____

8. $10 + $25 =$ _____

9. $150 \div 50 =$ _____

10. $50 + 50 =$ _____

11. $25 \times 7 =$ _____

12. $175 - 50 =$ _____

13. $75 \div 25 =$ _____

Units of Time

Complete each statement.

1. 1 d = _____ h   **2.** 1 h 48 min = _____ min   **3.** 3,600 s = _____ h

Add or subtract. Change to a larger unit when possible.

4.   3 h 15 min
         + 4 h 25 min
      _____

5.   6 h 36 min
         − 2 h 15 min
      _____

6.   4 h 25 min
         + 6 h 49 min
      _____

Find each elapsed time.

7. 7:15 A.M. to 1:45 P.M.

_____

8. 7:10 P.M. to 12:48 A.M.

_____

Problem Solving

9. It takes the school bus 40 minutes to complete the route from Gail's house to school. If Gail arrives at school at 8:10 A.M., what time does the bus pick her up?

_____

10. John has basketball practice four times per week. Each practice lasts 1 hour and

45 minutes. How many hours does John practice in all? _____

11. During lunch time, Joe's Deli typically sells about 20 sandwiches every hour. If lunch lasts from 11:15 A.M. to 2:45 P.M., about how many sandwiches are sold?

_____

Review and Remember

Find each answer.

12.   6,134
         + 2,486
      _____

13.   63,892
         − 6,083
      _____

14.   5,002
         − 1,398
      _____

15.   836
         ×   5
      _____

16.   235
         ×   4
      _____

17. 185 ÷ 60 = _____

18. 24.2 × 0.3 = _____

Customary Units of Length

Complete.

1. 36 ft = _____ yd

2. 29 in. = _____ ft _____ in.

3. 7 yd = _____ in.

4. 108 in. = _____ yd

Add or subtract. Change to a larger unit when possible.

5.   6 ft 2 in.
    + 4 ft 7 in.

6. 24 yd 1 ft 8 in.
    + 2 yd 2 ft 10 in.

7.   22 ft 7 in.
    − 14 ft 10 in.

8.   2 yd 1 ft
    −   2 ft

Problem Solving

9. Mrs. Rollins would like to put a border around her bulletin board. The bulletin board is shaped like a triangle with each side measuring 8 feet 4 inches. If the border comes in 6-foot strips, how many strips will she need? _____

10. Use a yardstick to measure the distance around your classroom. Use mental math to estimate the number of 6-foot strips that would be needed to place a border around

your room. _____

11. The length of the bedroom wall is 7 feet 5 inches. The closet along that wall is 3 feet 6 inches wide. Is there enough room along the wall to put a dresser that is 4 feet wide?

_____

Review and Remember

Compare. Use >, <, or =.

12. $6\frac{1}{2}$ ◯ $5\frac{3}{4}$

13. $3\frac{3}{4}$ ◯ $3\frac{2}{8}$

14. $6\frac{2}{3}$ ◯ $6\frac{7}{8}$

15. $5\frac{1}{2}$ ◯ $5\frac{3}{6}$

16. $4\frac{2}{3}$ ◯ $\frac{16}{3}$

17. $\frac{18}{8}$ ◯ $2\frac{1}{4}$

18. $\frac{64}{8}$ ◯ $\frac{16}{2}$

19. $2\frac{5}{8}$ ◯ $2\frac{6}{8}$

20. $3\frac{7}{8}$ ◯ $\frac{37}{8}$

Problem Solving

Is an Estimate Enough?

Answer each question. Explain your choices.

Michael is waiting for JB's annual spring sale. The skateboard he wants to buy costs $149.99. Last year the price of the board was $15.00 less. During the sale he hopes to save about 25%.

1. Which expression gives last year's price?

   a. $149.99 + $15.00 = $164.99

   b. $149.99 − $15.00 = $134.99

   c. $149.99 − $45.00 = $104.99

2. Which is true about this year's price increase?

   a. It was exactly $15.00.

   b. It was less than $15.00.

   c. It was more than $15.00.

3. Michael makes $10 for each lawn that he mows. He would like to know how many lawns he needs to mow to have enough money for the skateboard. Does he need an exact answer, or can he estimate how many lawns he needs to mow?

_____

_____

_____

Review and Remember

Complete the tables.

Rule: Add $3\frac{1}{2}$	
Input	**Output**
4. $2\frac{1}{2}$	
5.	$5\frac{1}{2}$
6. $3\frac{1}{4}$	
7. $1\frac{7}{8}$	

Rule: _____	
Input	**Output**
8. 4.5	2.2
9. 6.1	3.8
10.	4.7
11. 7.8	

Name _____

Customary Units of Capacity

Complete.

1. 1 gal = _____ qt

2. 128 fl oz = _____ gal

3. 3 gal = _____ pt

4. $8\frac{1}{2}$ pt = _____ cups

5. 3 qt = _____ fl oz

6. 15 qt = _____ gal

7. 1 gal = _____ cups

8. $3\frac{1}{2}$ qt = _____ cups

9. 4 gal = _____ qt

Problem Solving

10. The annual School Fair will be attended by 325 students. Each student will be served an 8-ounce cup of juice. Will 20 gallons of juice be enough to serve all of the students? Explain your answer.

_____

_____

11. Sarah is buying 4 extra gallons of juice for the fair. The juice sells for $0.79 per quart.

How much change will Sarah receive from $20.00? _____

12. You have a 1-cup container, a 1-pint container, and a 1-quart container. Is it possible

for you to measure out $1\frac{3}{8}$ gallons of liquid? Explain. _____

_____

_____

Review and Remember
Find each answer.

13. $64 \times 12 =$ _____

14. $128 \div 64 =$ _____

15. $1,483 - 695 =$ _____

16. $1.68 + 35.8 + 26 =$ _____

17. $34.1 - 4.69 =$ _____

18. $260 \times 3,000 =$ _____

19. $2,385 \times 203 =$ _____

20. $50 \times 20 \times 15 =$ _____

21. $6,464 \div 16 =$ _____

Customary Units of Weight

Complete.

1. 40 lb = _____ oz

2. 128 oz = _____ lb

3. 3 tons = _____ oz

4. 6 lb 3 oz = _____ oz

5. 200 oz = _____ lb _____ oz

6. 1 ton 3 lb = _____ lb

Problem Solving

Use the prices at the right to answer
Problems 7–8.

7. There are 320 children at the Fourth
of July picnic. If each child is going to
be served a 4-ounce hamburger, how
much hamburger meat does the com-
mittee need to buy? How much will
they spend?

A&B Market	
Item	Price
1 lb hamburger	$1.89
head of lettuce	$0.89
1 lb tomatoes	$1.19
1 lb onions	$0.89

_____

8. Mrs. Rosario plans to buy 128 oz of hamburger, three heads of lettuce, and 2 pounds
of tomatoes. Will her bill come to more than $20.00? Explain your answer.

_____

_____

Review and Remember

Find the mean, median, mode, and range of the following sets of numbers.

9. 14, 16, 25, 11

10. 300, 200, 300, 300, 4,000

11. $75, $75, $60

12. 1, 2, 3, 4, 5, 6, 7, 8, 9

13. 84, 78, 96, 78, 78, 78

14. 67, 48, 75, 82, 73

15. $2,000, $3,000, $5,000, $10,000, $7,000

Metric Units of Length

Complete.

1. 30 mm = _____ cm   **2.** 4,603 mm = _____ m   **3.** 460 m = _____ km

4. 0.03 km = _____ m   **5.** 1.73 m = _____ mm   **6.** 1.2 m = _____ mm

7. 400 cm = _____ m   **8.** 56 dm = _____ m   **9.** 8.4 m = _____ cm

Problem Solving

10. Marcia needs 15 meters of lace to finish making her curtains. She has to cut the lace

into 30-centimeter strips. How many strips will she cut? _____

11. The distance from Matthew's house to school is 2 kilometers. How many meters

does he walk to and from school in one week? _____

12. Myrna and Marty live 2,300 meters from each other. Myrna says that she lives 23

kilometers from Marty. Is she correct? Explain. _____

_____

_____

13. If Marty walked to Myrna's house and back, how many centimeters will he have

walked? _____

Review and Remember

Use mental math to find each answer.

14. 12,000 × 400 = _____   **15.** 3,200 × 30 = _____

16. 40,000 × 2,000 = _____   **17.** 11 × 5,000 = _____

18. 16,000 ÷ 4,000 = _____   **19.** 93,000,000 ÷ 3,000 = _____

20. 4,800 ÷ 800 = _____   **21.** 770,000 ÷ 1,100 = _____

22. 120,000 × 40 = _____   **23.** 5,100 × 200 = _____

Name _____

Metric Units of Capacity

Select the most reasonable metric unit of capacity for each.
Use mL or L.

1. glass of juice _____   **2.** pail of water _____   **3.** raindrop _____

4. can of soda _____   **5.** teaspoon of vanilla _____   **6.** mug of coffee _____

7. pot of coffee _____   **8.** jug of lemonade _____   **9.** dose of medicine _____

Problem Solving

10. Sarah bought four 2-liter bottles of juice for a party. She and her friends each had two cups of juice. If each cup held 200 mL of juice, how many friends did Sarah

serve? _____

11. Bob used three liquids for his science experiment. He used 285 mL of liquid A, 459 mL of liquid B, and 194 mL of liquid C. How much liquid did he use in all? Change to

larger units if possible. _____

12. Tung said that 3.8 liters of water is less than 38,000 milliliters of water. Henry said that they are the same amount. Who is correct? Explain.

_____

13. Bill needs 10.2 liters of soda for his party. He only has 7.3 liters. How many more

milliliters of soda does he need? _____

Review and Remember

Compare. Use $>$, $<$, and $=$.

14. 648 $\bigcirc$ 589.5   **15.** 16.30 $\bigcirc$ 16.3   **16.** 1.0080 $\bigcirc$ 10.080

17. 26×1 $\bigcirc$ $26 \div 1$ **18.** $3\frac{1}{2}$ $\bigcirc$ $3\frac{3}{4}$ **19.** $5\frac{3}{6}$ $\bigcirc$ $5\frac{4}{8}$

20. $\frac{8}{9}$ $\bigcirc$ $\frac{2}{3}$ **21.** $380 - 20$ $\bigcirc$ $380 - 10$ **22.** 35.1 $\bigcirc$ 35.11

Name _____

Metric Units of Mass

Select the most reasonable metric unit of mass for each.
Use mg, g, or kg.

1. kitten _____   **2.** automobile _____   **3.** toothbrush _____

4. fifth grader _____   **5.** feather _____   **6.** hot dog _____

7. bicycle _____   **8.** quarter _____   **9.** pot of gold _____

Problem Solving

10. In science class, students are asked to do an experiment using 75 grams of salt. If the class has two kilograms of salt, how many students will be able to do the experiment? _____

11. Shauna has an ear infection. She is taking 500 milligrams of medicine three times each day. How many grams of medicine will she take in ten days?

_____

12. Which has a greater mass: 2,200 grams of feathers or 2.2 kilograms of lead?

_____

13. A bag of rice has a mass of 600 grams. How many kilograms of rice are in 6 bags?

_____

Review and Remember

Write each improper fraction as a mixed number.

14. $\frac{8}{5}$ _____   **15.** $\frac{13}{7}$ _____   **16.** $\frac{24}{5}$ _____   **17.** $\frac{55}{7}$ _____

Write each mixed number as an improper fraction.

18. $4\frac{2}{5}$ _____   **19.** $10\frac{3}{8}$ _____   **20.** $2\frac{1}{5}$ _____   **21.** $3\frac{6}{11}$ _____

Ceisius and Fahrenheit Temperatures

Write the temperature for each thermometer.
Write an outdoor activity for each temperature.

1.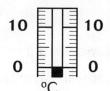

_____

_____

2.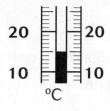

_____

_____

3.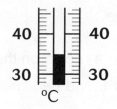

_____

_____

4.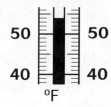

_____

_____

5.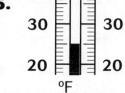

_____

_____

6.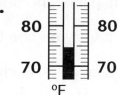

_____

_____

7.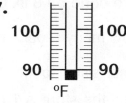

_____

_____

8.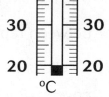

_____

_____

Problem Solving

Use the table at the right to answer Problems 9–10.

9. What will be the range of high and low temperature in Albany?

_____

10. How much warmer will the high temperature be in Atlanta than in Anchorage?

_____

Traveler's Forecast			
City	High (°F)	Low (°F)	Forecast
Albany	60	33	cloudy
Anchorage	40	29	cloudy
Atlanta	70	45	clear
Atlantic City	65	37	cloudy
Baltimore	64	39	cloudy
Buffalo	53	40	cloudy

Review and Remember

Find each answer.

11. $\frac{2}{7} \times 21 =$ _____

12. $64 \times \frac{3}{8} =$ _____

13. $\frac{4}{9} \times 72 =$ _____

Problem Solving

Use a Simulation

Use a simulation to solve.

1. Mr. Combs assigned a report on the United States. In one week Hayley had finished $\frac{1}{5}$ of her report. Her friend had finished $\frac{1}{6}$ of hers. How much longer will Hayley's friend need than Hayley to complete the report? _____

2. Mr. Combs plans to display the reports on bulletin boards. Each board is 5 ft by 9 ft. If the reports are done on 8 in. by 11 in. paper and he leaves a 2-in. space between reports, how many reports can he display on one board? _____

3. Giselle is wheeling her sister to the store in a carriage. Each turn of a carriage wheel covers 18 inches and the store is 1 mile away. How many times will the wheel turn before Giselle reaches the store? _____

4. Isabel and her friends have a lemonade stand. They bought 6 packages of lemonade mix at a price of 4 for $1.00 and 100 8-oz cups for $1.99. Each package of mix makes 4 quarts. If they sell each cupful of lemonade for $0.50, how much profit will they make? _____

Review and Remember

Solve each.

5. $\frac{3}{4} \times \frac{5}{9} =$ _____

6. $4\frac{2}{3} \times 2 =$ _____

7. $2\frac{2}{5} \times 1\frac{5}{6} =$ _____

8. $8 \times \frac{5}{8} =$ _____

9. $3\frac{3}{4} \times 1\frac{3}{5} =$ _____

10. $\frac{15}{26} \times \frac{8}{21} =$ _____

11. $2\frac{1}{2} \times 2\frac{1}{2} =$ _____

12. $1\frac{3}{8} \times 16 =$ _____

13. $3\frac{1}{3} \times \frac{2}{5} =$ _____

Perimeter

Find the perimeter of each figure.

1.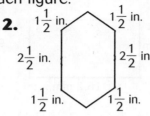

2.6 cm

4.8 cm

3.4 cm

2.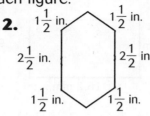

$1\frac{1}{2}$ in. $1\frac{1}{2}$ in.

$2\frac{1}{2}$ in. $2\frac{1}{2}$ in.

$1\frac{1}{2}$ in. $1\frac{1}{2}$ in.

3.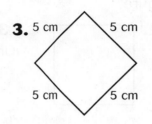

5 cm   5 cm

5 cm   5 cm

4.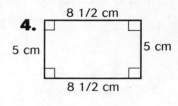

8 1/2 cm

5 cm   5 cm

8 1/2 cm

_____   _____   _____

Find each missing measurement.

5.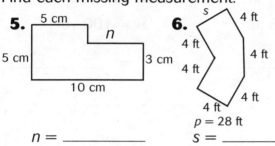

5 cm

n

5 cm   3 cm

10 cm

6.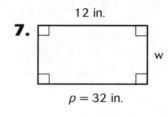

s   4 ft

4 ft

4 ft   4 ft

4 ft   4 ft

4 ft

p = 28 ft

7.

12 in.

w

p = 32 in.

8.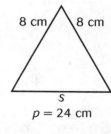

8 cm   8 cm

s

p = 24 cm

n = _____   s = _____   w = _____   s = _____

Problem Solving

9. Sam has a rectangular garden. The garden is twice as long as it is wide. If the perimeter of the garden is 60 yards, what are the length and width of the garden? Make a drawing.

_____

10. What are three possible dimensions of a rectangular garden with a perimeter of 40 yards? Use only whole numbers.

_____

_____

Review and Remember

Find each answer.

11.   0.4
    × 0.6

12.   0.27
    × 0.8

13.   2.4
    × 0.6

14.   49
    × 0.8

15. $0.23 \times 0.5 =$ _____

16. $0.8 \times 0.8 =$ _____

17. $0.5 \times 0.12 =$ _____

18. $0.25 \times 0.06 =$ _____

Area of Rectangles and Squares

Find the area of each figure.

1.

6 in.

3 in.

2.

3.8 ft

3.

4.8 mm

16.2 mm

4.

9 cm

3.2 cm

_____

_____

_____

_____

5. *l* = 16 ft

w = 8 ft

A = _____

6. *s* = 10 in.

A = _____

7. *l* = $5\frac{1}{2}$ in.

w = 6 in.

A = _____

8. *l* = 100 yd

w = 100 yd

A = _____

Problem Solving

9. Mr. Conroy is planting grass in his front yard. His yard measures 15 feet by 24 feet. Each bag of seed covers 400–500 square feet. Is one bag of seed enough? Show

your work. _____

10. Mr. Conroy's back yard is twice as long and twice as wide as his front yard. How many bags of seed would he need for his back yard? Make a drawing to explain your

answer. _____

11. Mrs. Kessler has a yard that is the same area as Mr. Conroy's front yard. Her front yard is 2 feet longer than it is wide. What are the dimensions of Mrs. Kessler's

front yard? _____

Review and Remember

Find each answer.

12. $\frac{3}{5} \times \frac{10}{27} =$ _____

13. $\frac{1}{2} \times 8 =$ _____

14. $\frac{4}{9} \times \frac{15}{16} =$ _____

15. $2\frac{1}{2} \times 2\frac{1}{2} =$ _____

16. $3\frac{1}{2} \times 4\frac{2}{5} =$ _____

17. $4\frac{2}{3} \times \frac{9}{28} =$ _____

18. $10\frac{2}{3} \times 1\frac{7}{8} =$ _____

19. $16 \times \frac{1}{32} =$ _____

20. $\frac{4}{5} \times 1\frac{2}{7} =$ _____

Name _____

Area of Parallelograms and Triangles

Find the area of each figure.

1.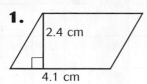
2.4 cm
4.1 cm

2.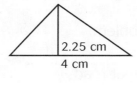
2.25 cm
4 cm

3.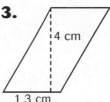
4 cm
1.3 cm

4.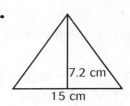
7.2 cm
15 cm

_____ _____ _____ _____

Find each missing measurement.

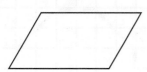  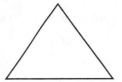 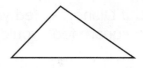

5. $b = 2$ in.

$h =$ _____

$A = 3$ in.²

6. $b = 2.6$ cm

$h = 5.7$ cm

$A =$ _____

7. $b = 20$ m

$h =$ _____

$A = 100$ m²

8. $b =$ _____

$h = 4$ ft

$A = 7$ ft²

Problem Solving

Use the drawing at the right to answer Problems 9–10.

9. The drawing shows a new parking lot that is about to be paved. How large is the area being paved?

_____

10. Fencing costs $2.00 per foot. How much will it cost to place

a fence around the entire lot? _____

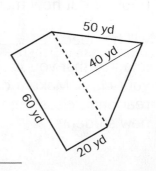
50 yd
40 yd
60 yd
20 yd

Review and Remember

Find the answer.

11. $3\frac{3}{8} + 4\frac{5}{8} =$ _____

12. $6\frac{2}{3} + 4\frac{2}{3} =$ _____

13. $6\frac{2}{4} + 4\frac{5}{6} =$ _____

14. $5\frac{3}{5} - 2\frac{1}{3} =$ _____

15. $6\frac{3}{4} - 2\frac{1}{4} =$ _____

16. $8\frac{1}{4} - 6 =$ _____

Problem Solving
Area of Irregular Polygons

Use the diagrams at the right to solve each problem.

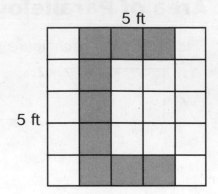

5 ft

5 ft

1. Diane is painting the letters of a large sign that reads CLASS OF 1997. Each letter and number is 5 ft high. About how many square feet of area will she paint to complete the sign? _____

_____

2. If Diane painted your name in 5-ft letters, how many square feet would the paint cover?

_____

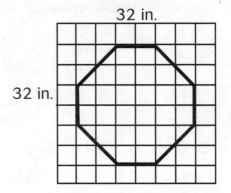

32 in.

32 in.

3. Steve wants to paint a stop sign on his bedroom door. Use the diagram at the right to find the

area of the sign. _____

_____

4. Joshua is buying a cover for his swimming pool. About how many square feet of material

will he need? _____

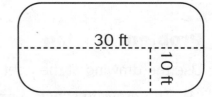

30 ft

10 ft

5. Imagine that you have five new students coming into your class. Make a drawing that shows how you could rearrange classroom furniture to make space for the new students.

Review and Remember

Estimate each answer. Then divide.

6. 8)6,384   **7.** 3)20,645   **8.** 9)4,823   **9.** 4)18,392

EXPLORE: Volume

Find each missing measurement.

1. $l = 2$ ft

$w = 3$ ft

$h = 4$ ft

$V =$ _____

2. $l = 1.3$ in.

$w = 2.6$ in.

$h = 1.3$ in.

$V =$ _____

3. $l = 4.5$ m

$w = 4$ m

$h = 5.2$ m

$V =$ _____

4. $l = 6\frac{1}{2}$ yd

$w = 4\frac{2}{3}$ yd

$h = 2\frac{1}{7}$ yd

$V =$ _____

5. $l =$ _____

$w = 15$ cm

$h = 10$ cm

$V = 3,000$ cm³

6. $l = 8$ m

$w =$ _____

$h = 9$ m

$V = 396$ m³

7. $l = 7$ m

$w = 7$ m

$h =$ _____

$V = 343$ m³

8. $l = 6.4$ cm

$w = 2.2$ cm

$h = 3.0$ cm

$V =$ _____

Problem Solving

9. Mr. Clifford has a rectangular swimming pool that is 5 feet deep, 36 feet long, and

24 feet wide. What is the volume of his pool? _____

10. Mr. Clifford is thinking about buying a plastic cover for his pool. If the cover costs

$0.50 per square foot, how much will it cost to buy the cover? _____

11. Mr. David has a pool that has the same volume as Mr. Clifford's pool. Mr. David's pool is 10 feet deep. What are some possible dimensions of Mr. David's pool?

_____

Review and Remember

Solve.

12. $4,368 \div 25 =$ _____

13. $95 \times 35 =$ _____

14. $36 \times (4 + 6) =$ _____

15. $204 \times 103 =$ _____

16. $16 + 2 \times 3 - 10 =$ _____

17. $15 - 6 + 3 - 2 =$ _____

18. $(3 \times 2) + (4 \times 8) =$ _____

19. $7 - 6 \div 2 + 4 =$ _____

Understanding Ratios

Write each ratio in two different ways.

1. 3:6 _____

2. seven to eight _____

3. $\frac{16}{29}$ _____

4. 4 to 5 _____

Make a drawing for each ratio. Use color, shape, or size to show ratio.

5. $\frac{5}{3}$

6. 7:9

Problem Solving

7. Ivy thinks that the ratio 2:1 is the same as 4:2. Do you agree? Make a drawing to

explain your answer. _____

8. Bud thinks that the ratio of dimes to one dollar is 5:1. Do you agree or disagree?

Why? _____

_____

Review and Remember

Find each answer. Write each fraction in simplest form.

9. $2 - \frac{1}{5} =$ _____

10. $\frac{1}{8} + 64 =$ _____

11. $4\frac{1}{8} \times 3 =$ _____

12. $5.08 \times 0.9 =$ _____

Equivalent Ratios

Complete each ratio table.

1.

5	10			
7		21	28	

2.

2		6		
6	12			30

3.

3		9	12		18
10	20			50	

4.

4		12		
11			44	

Write three ratios that are equivalent to each given ratio.

5. 2:4 _____

6. $\frac{3}{9}$ _____

7. 15:30 _____

8. $\frac{4}{28}$ _____

Problem Solving

9. If six out of seven tires in one shipment were returned as defective, and 14 tires were shipped, how many were returned? _____

10. Inspectors check $\frac{4}{5}$ of the tires in a batch. If an inspector checks 400 tires in one batch, how many tires did she *not* inspect in the batch? _____

Review and Remember

Find each answer.

11. $5.08 \times 3 =$ _____

12. $45.2 \div 2 =$ _____

13. $6.1 - 3.9 =$ _____

14. $7.8 - 0.81 =$ _____

15. $61 \times 1.4 =$ _____

16. $3.08 \div 4 =$ _____

Exploring Scale Drawing

Find the model size or actual size of each object.

1.

Width of model	2 in.	4 in.	
Actual width	8 ft		24 ft

2.

Length of model	6 in.		18 in.
Actual length	24 mi.	48 mi.	

3.

Width of model	3 in.	6 in.	
Actual width	10 in.		30 in.

4.

Length of model	5 m		15 m
Actual length	15 km	30 km	

Find the model size or the actual size of each object.

5. $\dfrac{4 \text{ in.}}{6 \text{ ft.}} = \dfrac{\rule{1cm}{0.4pt}}{36 \text{ ft.}}$

6. $\dfrac{\rule{1cm}{0.4pt}}{1.1 \text{ m}} = \dfrac{2 \text{ cm}}{2.2 \text{ m}}$

Problem Solving

7. An artist is painting a picture from a photograph. Two inches on the photograph equals 1 foot on the painting. The photograph is 4 in. × 6 in. What will the size of the painting be? _____

8. The scale on a road map is 1 inch to 20 miles. About how many miles long is a road that is approximately 5.5 inches long on the map? _____

9. The scale on a blueprint is 1 cm to 2m. How wide is an office that is 1.5 cm wide on the blueprint? _____

Review and Remember

Add or subtract.

10. $3\frac{2}{9} + 4\frac{7}{9} =$

11. $4\frac{1}{3} - \frac{2}{3} =$

12. $6\frac{1}{2} + \frac{1}{6} =$

_____   _____   _____

Understanding Rates

Use equivalent ratios or division to complete.

1. 3 gallons of milk for $6.69

    1 gallon of milk for _____

2. 4 containers of yogurt for $2.76

    1 container of yogurt for _____

3. 150 miles in 3 hours

    _____ miles in 1 hour

4. 3 books for $3.99

    1 book for _____

Problem Solving

Use equivalent ratios to solve Problems 5–8.

5. If 144 science kits cost $1,296.00, then how much do one dozen kits cost?

_____

6. A three-day hike covers 60 miles. About how far do the hikers travel each day?

_____

7. A 4-piece set of dishes costs $15.95. How much do 4 sets cost?

_____

8. If it takes you 10 minutes to read 8 pages of a book, can you read

64 pages in an hour? Explain. _____

_____

Review and Remember

Write the place value of each underlined digit.

9. 5̲6,798

_____

10. 1̲34,465,987

_____

11. 4̲,908,663,898

_____

12. 82,3̲10

_____

13. 9,23̲8,416

_____

14. 7,7̲77,777

_____

Problem Solving
Choose the Operation

Answer each question. Give a reason for your choice.

Joanna made a $25 down payment on a television set that cost $250. She agreed to pay the balance in 9 equal monthly payments. How much is each payment?

1. Which represents the amount Joanna still owes?

  a. $250.00

  b. $250 − $25

  c. $250 ÷ 9

2. Which statement describes her monthly payments?

  a. The cost of the television divided by the number

  of payments.

  b. The down payment subtracted from the cost of

  the television.

  c. The down payment subtracted from the cost of the television

  and the difference divided by the number of payments.

3. Which number sentence represents the amount of each monthly payment?

  a. $250 ÷ 9 = $27.78

  b. $250 − $25 = $225

  c. ($250 − $25) ÷ 9 = $25

Review and Remember

Find the Greatest Common Factor.

4. 32 and 56   **5.** 24 and 36   **6.** 140 and 150   **7.** 16 and 24

_____   _____   _____   _____

Find the Least Common Multiple.

8. 14 and 21   **9.** 16 and 24   **10.** 18 and 21   **11.** 24 and 36

_____   _____   _____   _____

EXPLORE: Understanding Percent

Write each percent as a ratio.

1. 70% _____   **2.** 68% _____

3. 85% _____   **4.** 12% _____

Write each ratio as a percent. Use grid paper if you wish.

5. $\frac{23}{100}$ _____   **6.** 2 out of 5 _____

7. $\frac{40}{40}$ _____   **8.** $\frac{3}{5}$ _____

Problem Solving

9. Thirty-five out of each 100 students in the Pine Tree Middle School can attend the

Harmony Festival. What percent of students can attend? _____

10. Five out of 10 batteries need to be replaced each year.

What percent of the batteries are replaced? _____

11. Three out of each 10 basketball players in the Central City School District are taller

than 6 ft 6 in. What percent of the players are *shorter* than 6 ft 6 in.? _____

12. If 25 out of 50 dogs in the Eastminster Dog Show are owned by women, what

percent are owned by men? _____

Review and Remember

Add or subtract.

13. 5.90 + 3.19 = _____   **14.** 1.34 − 0.46 = _____

15. 4.908 + 66 = _____   **16.** 75.3 − 1.75 = _____

Relating Percents, Decimals, and Fractions

Write each percent as a decimal and as a fraction in simplest form.

1. 20% _____

2. 32% _____

3. 29% _____

4. 46% _____

Write each expression in two other ways.

5. 57% _____

6. 0.79 _____

7. 20/20 _____

8. 0.05 _____

Problem Solving

9. Draw a 10 × 10 grid. Shade 24% of the squares. What percent is not shaded?

_____

10. A design has 100 triangles. Forty percent of the triangles are solid colors. Of these

triangles, 10 are blue. How many solid-colored triangles are not blue? _____

Review and Remember

Find each answer.

11.   4.6
       × 3

12.   4,351
          2.6
       + 3.46

13.   4.9
       × 7

Problem Solving
Use Logical Reasoning

Solve.

1. Marissa's little brother made a tower of blocks 10 rows high. There are 19 blocks on the bottom row, 17 in the second row, and so on. How many blocks are in

the tower? _____

2. A donkey and a mule were carrying bags of corn. If the mule gave the donkey one bag, they would have the same number. If the donkey gave the mule one bag, the mule would have twice as many bags as the donkey. How many bags is each carrying?

_____

3. Farmer Green sent his two children out to count the hens and sheep. His daughter counted 40 heads, and his son counted 100 legs. How many of each animal is

on the farm? _____

4. You have two pails. One holds 4 gallons. The other holds 7 gallons. How can you go to the lake and bring

back exactly five gallons of water? _____

_____

_____

Review and Remember

Find each answer.

5. $3\frac{3}{5} \times 5$

6. $2\frac{4}{7} \times 5\frac{5}{6}$

7. $2\frac{1}{4} - 1\frac{1}{3}$

8. $3\frac{1}{3} + 2\frac{1}{4}$

9. $\frac{5}{8} - \frac{3}{5} + \frac{2}{10}$

10. $7\frac{3}{5} + 2\frac{5}{6}$

EXPLORE: Understanding Probability

Write *greater* chance or *lesser* chance to make each statement true.

1. There are 25 red beans and 10 blue beans in a jar. You have a

_____ chance of choosing a red bean.

2. Sixty-five names are in a hat. There are 25 boy's names and 40

girl's names. There is a _____ chance that a boy's

name will be drawn.

3. You are drawing shapes from a container. There are 10

round shapes and 12 square shapes. You have a

_____ chance of drawing a square.

Problem Solving

4. Amal earns 7% each year on money in his bank account. If he has

$100.00 in the bank, how much interest will he earn in one year? _____

5. Caeti has designed a mathematics game where players draw numbers from a hat.

There are 14 two-digit numbers and 12 three-digit numbers. Are players more likely to

draw a two-digit number or a three-digit number, if the numbers are replaced in the

bag after each turn? Why?

_____

_____

Review and Remember

Write the value of the underlined digit.

6. 4.<u>62</u>   **7.** <u>4</u>.6   **8.** 4.9<u>1</u>

_____   _____   _____

Finding Probability

A bag contains 25 cards numbered 1–25. You pick a card.
After you pick a card, you return it to the bag.
Find each probability.

1. 4

_____

2. a number in the 20s

_____

3. a number with a 3

_____

4. a number in the hundreds

_____

5. an odd number

_____

6. a number with a zero

_____

7. an even number

_____

8. a number with a 2

_____

Problem Solving

9. The probability of choosing a blue hat from a bag is $\frac{4}{10}$. How many blue hats are in

the bag? How many hats of other colors? _____

10. There are 6 blue beads in a case and 9 green beads. What is the probability of choosing a blue bead from the case?

_____

11. A spinner is divided into 4 equal sections. Two sections are red, and 2 sections are green. What is the probability of spinning red? Of spinning yellow?

_____

Review and Remember

Find each answer. Round to the nearest thousandth.

12. $4.33 \times 2.2 =$ _____

13. $23.5 \times 4 =$ _____

14. $14.25 \div 2.3 =$ _____

Fair and Unfair Games

The faces of a cube are numbered 1–6. Each player rolls the number cube two times and finds the sum of the rolls. Each player must follow his or her rule under "What wins." Decide if each game described below is fair or unfair. Explain.

	Player	What Wins	Fair or Unfair
1.	A	sums are even numbers	
	B	sums are odd numbers	
2.	A	sums < 10	
	B	sums > 10	
3.	A	sums with a zero in any place	
	B	sums with a zero in the ones place	
4.	A	sums are a whole number	
	B	sums are not a fraction	

Problem Solving

5. Sarina thinks her mathematics game is fair because each player has the same number of draws. How would you explain to Sarina that the number of draws is not all that is required for a fair game?

_____

_____

6. You are buying games for a car trip. Three hand-held games cost $3.49 each, and one magnetic board game costs $5.49. You have $20. Can you buy all four games? If not, how much more money do you need? If so, how much change will you receive?

_____

Review and Remember

Find each answer.

7. 43,201 − 459 = _____   **8.** 231.5 + 4.09 = _____   **9.** 104.25 − 2.3 = _____

Tree Diagrams

1. Make a tree diagram to show the possible outcomes
of picking a crayon and a fruit.

2. Make a tree diagram to show the outcomes of picking
a crayon and a shape.

3. What is the probability of choosing a blue crayon? _____

Problem Solving

4. Jake bought popcorn at the fair with 8 coins.
The popcorn cost 69¢. What coins might he
have used? _____

5. Three toppings can be put on any one of four
flavors of ice cream. How many combinations
can be made? _____

Review and Remember

Compare. Write >, <, or = .

6. 75 ÷ 5 ◯ 30 ÷ 2   **7.** 894 + 321 ◯ 1,325 − 198   **8.** 20.3 × 5 ◯ 100 + 25

Use with Grade 5, text pages 502-503. **149**

Problem Solving
Using Circle Graphs

Use the circle graph at the right for Problems 1–5.

1. How much greater percentage of time was spent watching comedies than watching game shows? _____

2. What type of television program seems to be the most popular? _____

3. If each percent represents one-half hour of TV viewing, how much time is spent watching sports? _____

4. What percent of time was spent watching soap operas? _____

5. Write your own word problem, using information from the circle graph.

TV Survey Results

Soap Operas

Game Shows 25%

Comedies 32%

Movies 10%

Sports 14%

6. What type of TV shows do you watch? Estimate the number of hours for each type of show. Then make a circle graph to represent your TV viewing.

Review and Remember

Find each answer.

7. 1.95
    6.25
  + 8.04

8. 23
    4.85
  + 0.09

9. $26.51
  − 4.51

10.   8.04
    − 0.006

11. 3.85×0.02

12. 34.5×1.23

13. $16.45 \div 0.5$

14. $2.1 \div 0.5$